Awakening

to the

Fifth Dimension

A Guide for Navigating the Global Shift

First Edition Design Publishing

Awakening to the Fifth Dimension
Copyright ©2014 Vidya Frazier

ISBN 978-1622-876-29-7 PRINT
ISBN 978-1622-876-30-3 EBOOK

LCCN 2014940840

May 2014

Published and Distributed by
First Edition Design Publishing, Inc.
P.O. Box 20217, Sarasota, FL 34276-3217
www.firsteditiondesignpublishing.com

Awakening
to the
Fifth Dimension

A Guide for
Navigating the
Global Shift

Vidya Frazier

Table of Contents

Preface

I first felt inspired to write this book back in 2011 when I began hearing people around me speaking of all the profound changes happening in the world and in their own lives. I heard the excitement in their voices when they would talk about the "Shift" they saw occurring on the planet and what might be happening in 2012.

Yet underneath all the excitement, I was also hearing a subtext of stress and fear that many were experiencing because of the changes they were seeing and feeling. I sensed their insecurity as they experienced the ground beneath their feet rapidly shifting in many areas of their lives.

I too was experiencing deep changes in my own life. And I too was watching important shifts taking place on the planet and wondering with some trepidation where they could all be leading. But I realized how fortunate I was, because I had a context in which to put all that was happening—a context that brought tremendous joy and optimism to my heart.

Ascension and the Fifth Dimension

This context was a paradigm known as "Ascension". The teachings about Ascension speak of a Golden Age the planet earth is now moving toward and an amazing world-wide awakening that will be taking us into that age. They describe how we will be shifting from the level of consciousness we currently function at to a higher one that's been named the "Fifth Dimension". After a brief period of intense change, the earth will eventually become a place in which love, respect, peace and freedom reign.

I have to admit that when I first read about the ideas in this Ascension paradigm a number of years ago, I was rather dismissive of it. It seemed a flowery, airy-fairy notion born of some metaphysical dream—sweet but not realistic. I had lived through many decades of doing hard spiritual "work", studying traditions from both the East and the West, and such a simplistic view of an awakening of the masses, so to speak, just didn't seem plausible.

Indeed, it seemed clear to me that situations in the world seemed to be getting progressively worse every day; human suffering and ill will among nations were as widespread as ever. How could we possibly be approaching a Golden Age?

Yet much to my surprise, as time went by, I felt myself drawn more and more into exploring the ideas of this paradigm. Eventually I realized that it actually made sense of everything that appears to be happening currently, both in the world and within myself and many people I know.

But most of all, I realized I was simply resonating on a profound level with the ideas and experiences in the Ascension teachings. I was waking up to memories of the far distant past and also to intuitions about the future. I was experiencing deep yearnings to return to a home I had known at some time long ago—and I realized with great excitement that somehow I would soon be returning there.

At some point, the paradigm finally became a living reality within me. I knew without a doubt that whether we believed it or not, Ascension into a higher consciousness was actually occurring. It described exactly what was happening within and all around me.

Studying the Ascension Process

I realized I really wanted to study this process—from every source I could get my hands on. There weren't that many sources at the time (and there still aren't, although they're quickly increasing). Most sources were channelings—some of which I resonated with, and some not. Some were teachings of teachers who were out on the edge of metaphysical circles, offering esoteric teachings to small groups of people.

I learned a lot from these sources, but I realized that I mainly wanted to study what was happening within myself as I experienced the shifts of Ascension. I also wanted to observe people around me who were going through similar changes.

In addition, I began seeing indications of Ascension happening in the news, as well, as I saw numerous signs of an enormous shift taking place in the world: both the breakdown of old structures and systems and the birth of new and exciting ones.

Indeed, at times, I am moved to tears, as I witness the great numbers of people on the planet awakening. It's clear that much has to shift before a collective awakening can fully bring about a "New Earth". But if I look beyond what the mainstream media focuses on, I can easily see this new reality already unfolding.

As time has gone by, I've realized more and more that the teachings about Ascension offer a deeply satisfying explanation about what is happening now and what appears to be ahead of us. They also describe certain challenges we may face as we journey into the Fifth Dimension.

But most of all, these teachings have unlocked a place in my heart that experiences a profound joy that lies far beyond any sense of wishful thinking or hope of a better future: it is a joy born of a deep knowing of an undeniable truth. My entire being vibrates with this knowing.

In this book I wish to share what I have discovered about this journey I believe we are all making into fifth-dimensional consciousness. I draw on my own experiences and on inner teachings I have received from my guides, archangels working with me, and other celestial beings I inwardly communicate with.

I also draw on reports of friends, family members, clients and students, as well as on teachings of teachers and certain channels who speak about Ascension and the Fifth Dimension. I have designed the book to be a guide or map of the territory we are all now traversing as we approach this new reality.

What to Expect

The beginning chapters in the "Introduction" section will introduce you to the general paradigm of Ascension. They will describe the different dimensions or levels of consciousness we are experiencing—the one we are leaving behind, the one we are currently primarily experiencing, and the one we are moving toward.

The following chapters in the section called "Understanding the Ascension Process" will explore the myriad facets of Ascension many people are experiencing.

Some of the "symptoms" I describe in this section may seem somewhat challenging when you first read them. The experiences are actually symptomatic of what people often experience when any great change happens in their lives—which makes sense, as the process of Ascension will likely bring more change in our lives than we've ever had to live through before.

I suggest that in reading this section you not be discouraged. None of us much likes the process of change; often uncomfortable demands are made of us to let go of what feels safe and familiar. But if we can learn to trust and surrender to the process, and to consciously release what is no longer needed as we travel into higher consciousness, the changes we undergo can actually be joyful and profoundly fulfilling.

Also keep in mind that each of us is unique, and we are all going through this process in our own way. You may not resonate with everything described; some things may be very different for you. Indeed, the maturity and transformational work some bring to their Ascension process may allow for a gentler experience than for those just beginning to awaken their self-awareness.

Remember that it is important to validate your own experience, whatever it is. You may simply wish to use the descriptions I offer as reference points for understanding what other people around you may be experiencing. (Al - though they may also describe experiences you haven't yet had.)

The chapters in the final section, "Keys for Navigating the Ascension Process", focus on how to make the necessary shifts in consciousness with as much ease and grace as possible. And also how to fully enjoy this incredibly exciting ride we are all on, as we travel together toward the unknown shores of the Fifth Dimension.

I invite you to open your mind and simply take in what I present to see if you resonate with it. As much as you can, let go of your rational mind as you read and slip into a deeper place inside you that intuits truth when you meet it.

You may realize that what you're reading is actually nothing new to you—that you have known it all for eons of time. It's just now time for you to begin to remember.

Vidya Frazier,
May 2014

Introduction

Chapter 1
Reality is Shifting

We are living in extraordinary times. The world is changing politically, socially and technologically at such a rapid rate, it may soon be unrecognizable to most of us alive today.

We are also facing countless seemingly-unsolvable crises: over-population, polluted rain forests, global warming, rising unemployment, peak oil, global food shortages and starvation, poisoned oceans, and severe climate changes. And we watch as the world economy teeters on the verge of collapse.

To say we're living in uncertain times is an enormous understatement. We're facing possible global disasters on so many different fronts, it can seem the human race is heading for extinction.

Global Transformation

And yet, at the same time, if we look closely, we can see that very hopeful events and developments are also occurring, and that they're rapidly gaining momentum over time.

Great movements of people in numerous countries world-wide are now standing up and essentially saying "No more!" to those in power. They're protesting ever-increasing inequities in wealth and power, and age-old paradigms and structures based on greed, exploitation and patriarchal ideals. And they're beginning to bring them down.

The media, especially the alternative and international sources, are reporting unprecedented disclosures of corruption, greed and exploitation occurring within our political, social, religious and financial institutions. Whistleblowers everywhere are finding more and more courage to step forward, revealing the decay existing in these obsolete institutions.

Through these disclosures, people are witnessing a collapse of many of the collective lies that have been in our culture for thousands of years. They're seeing more and more behind the scenes, how they've been manipulated by those in power.

It's apparent that many across the world are experiencing a new sense of empowerment, asserting their desire for peace and respect for all beings on the planet. They're exposing dictators and the ruling elite, refusing to be suppressed any longer.

Growing numbers of groups are building their own local, sustainable industries over which they can have control, based on values of justice, compassion, and equality. New businesses are focusing on team-building and on "giving back". Grass roots inventors are creating and sharing their inventions for accessing free energy through simple technology that is almost cost-free.

Meanwhile, the internet is empowering and uniting people across the globe in ways never before possible in history. Millions are experiencing a sense of connection and unification. And, very significantly, women across the world are asserting their rights with a power and impact never before seen.

Children of the New Age

Another fascinating and hopeful phenomenon to watch is the emergence of the groups of children and young adults often referred to as the "Indigos", the "Crystals", and the "Star Children"—all who appear to hold no sense of limitation of what is possible in life.

Seemingly unburdened by humanity's failures of the past, these young people refuse to listen to fear-based admonitions from their elders about what is or isn't possible. They forge ahead under their own steam, apparently clear about what they want to create and experience, certain they can succeed through their own intentions.

Many of these children, especially the very young ones, are astounding people with their innate musical and artistic talents and abilities. The internet is filled with videos portraying very young children playing complicated musical compositions, with seemingly little or no learning. There are other young ones explaining complex theories of science or metaphysics that no one has taught them.

But perhaps most encouraging is how clear so many of these children and young adults are in their intentions for serving humankind with their talents and abilities. They don't appear to be motivated by age-old values of greed, competition or suppression.

Indeed, many of the young children continually astound the adults around them with statements of profound spiritual wisdom and clarity about what is just and fair and how the world should be run.

Some seem to have memories of having come from other places in the universe and speak clearly about what life is like where they come from. Others speak about lifetimes they've lived previously on the earth that can be verified through research.

A New Earth

In many ways, it seems that a new Earth is being born, a whole new era in which life on this planet promises to be quite different from what it has been since the beginning of history, one which many of us have dreamed of and longed for—a world filled with loving kindness, justice, peace and sense of oneness.

And yet it's clear that it will be a while before this new Earth can fully manifest. Some enormous and essential changes may be occurring for a while, posing some challenges for all of us.

Personal Transformation

Many of us have been sensing this same kind of accelerating and disquieting change happening in our personal lives as well. We have a feeling that life as we've known it is somehow slipping away, shifting dramatically and rapidly.

In particular, we're noticing that challenges and loss seem to be occurring in many areas of our lives—in our relationships, our work, our health, our financial situation. Somehow our old sense of identity seems to be disappearing—and with it, for some, a feeling of security.

Once-comfortable situations in our lives are now becoming less tolerable. Old-time friends seem to be on different wavelengths than we are, and certain family members are getting harder for us to be around. At times, old painful patterns we thought we healed years ago are suddenly arising again. Intense emotions seem to appear out of nowhere.

In general, we sometimes feel like we're being compelled to step into unknown territory where nothing in our life is predictable or certain anymore—including who we are.

And yet, paradoxically, at the same time, wonderful new experiences are also happening—ones filled with awakening, deep joy and freedom. At times, we feel an intense love rising up in us out of nowhere—for someone in particular, for the entire human race, for ourselves. Or even when in the midst of feeling a lonely separation from people, we somehow have a profound experience of oneness with all that exists.

More and more, synchronicity seems to abound in our lives. Deep happiness fills us at the strangest times, and a sweet peace steals over us for no apparent reason. We feel the presence of a magnificent divine Self arising within us, gently nudging our ego aside. And in deep, precious moments, we feel such an intense longing for *Home*—wherever and whatever that might be—that we are in tears.

The Shift

If you can relate to any of these powerful and sometimes puzzling experiences, know that you're not alone. You're one of a growing group of people on the planet today who are experiencing symptoms of what has been named *the Shift*.

In essence, you are in the process of a very rapid spiritual awakening—one that most traditional spiritual teachings don't mention because it's something unique to our time, something that has never before happened in history.

And yet, this shift of consciousness in the world and in our personal lives has actually been predicted for a long time by certain visionaries, spiritual teachers, astrologers and indigenous elders from traditions across the world. It is even alluded to in the New Testament.

One explanation of why the Shift is happening is that the earth has recently arrived at a new part of the galaxy—the middle of the Milky Way—something it does every 26,000 years. In this part of the galaxy, very high frequencies exist. And these frequencies are being absorbed into the world of matter, causing the vibratory rate of everything (including us) to lift and evolve very quickly.

Powerful changes are also currently occurring on the sun. Numerous, ongoing coronal mass ejections—massive bursts of solar wind and magnetic fields—are being released into space and flooding the earth. And these are impacting us as well.

Visionaries tell us that these cosmic events—along with others that are occurring across the whole galaxy—are causing more light to enter into matter and into consciousness, and that the rapid collective spiritual evolution that's beginning to manifest is in response to these frequencies.

This may sound like a wonderful thing to happen—and it is. But the process it entails—which includes the need to quickly let go of old patterns, beliefs, feelings, judgments and ideas of what reality is—can make life rocky, confusing and uncomfortable at times.

Indeed, the shifting of consciousness many of us are experiencing is not the kind of shift most of us are used to, one that moves us gently and gradually into a higher state of consciousness. This is a radical and monumental transformation that some are referring to as an *evolutionary leap of consciousness*—or the *birth of a whole new human species*.

What can make it especially challenging is the speed at which this shifting into a new level of consciousness seems to be taking place. Although many of us have been awakening in one way or another for a number of years, we're now at the point of the process where changes may begin accelerating very rapidly.

And this may at times cause a sense of disorientation, confusion and fear—both within us individually and in society as a whole—as old patterns of negativity and limitation are released and new higher energies are absorbed. Profound change like this, even if for the better, can sometimes be quite challenging.

Transitional Times

Indigenous elders tell us that during the next decade or so, we will be experiencing what they have named the

"Transitional Times" or "In-Between Times". The old tired structures and paradigms that have been fueled by corruption, control and greed for ages of time are now beginning to seriously crumble—and that which will replace them has not yet fully arrived.

It's difficult to know at this point how accurate these predictions are for these coming times—or how severe the disruptions may be. But it seems clear that, at least to some degree, we may see increasing confusion and uncertainty as people struggle to adjust to the changing reality around them.

Most people are still in denial about the profound changes taking place in the world. They're not putting the puzzle pieces together, not seeing how the planet is actually in crisis—and may well be there for a while before a new world can arise out of it. But the truth of what's happening is undeniable, however people may choose to understand and contextualize it.

Ushering in the Shift

Taking in the seriousness of what is happening on the planet is essential to be able to make it through the times ahead with a sense of equanimity. But it's also important to not react to it all with fear or anger.

This is a time rather to become prepared—both spiritually and otherwise—so we can be as clear, steady, and awake as possible to navigate our way through the coming times with balance and ease. And it's a time for those of us who feel called, to step forward to do what we have come here to do this lifetime to help usher in this new and transformational era of human life.

If you resonate with these ideas, chances are you understood very clearly before you incarnated this lifetime what these times were going to be about—and that you volunteered to be one of the way showers through these transitional times.

Navigating the Transitional Times

But how to do this during those times when rapid and confusing changes are taking place within your life and all around you? This book is a guide designed to help you in this process, to assist you in crossing the sometimes tumultuous waters of these times ahead with as much ease and clarity as possible.

It's also designed to help remind you, no matter what may be going on, of the big picture of what's happening—the incredible transformation we are experiencing as we courageously take this extraordinary evolutionary leap into higher consciousness.

As you take this leap, you may see that something wondrous and breath-taking is happening: you are finally finding your way back to the Home you have yearned for in the most intimate depths of your being, perhaps for as long as you can remember.

Chapter 2
Ascension into the Fifth Dimension

One of the most helpful ways to understand the Shift is to put it into the context of a dimensional shift—a movement we're making from one dimension (or level) of consciousness to another. The process of this dimensional shift has been called *Ascension.*

Within this paradigm, the shift we're making is from the level of consciousness called the "Third Dimension" into the level known as the "Fifth Dimension". The bridge between these two realities, the one we're currently crossing, is the "Fourth Dimension".

Much has been written, spoken and channeled about the Ascension process and the Fifth Dimension. Although not every source agrees on details about this higher realm of reality, most do describe similar major characteristics.

A Utopian Dream?

In general, the Fifth Dimension has been described as a level of reality in which a consciousness of love, peace, and spiritual wisdom prevails. In fact, much of what has been described about this dimension can sound to the rational mind like a utopian dream or a fairy tale.

For instance, most sources agree that once the final shift into the Fifth Dimension takes place, all people on Earth will be living in peace and harmony, experiencing oneness with all of life, fully respecting all people and the earth itself and communicating with love and understanding. Fear, hunger, poverty and crime will all be obsolete. There will be equality, justice, respect and abundance for all.

And everyone will be awake to the majestic, divine multi-dimensional beings they actually are.

Magical Thinking, Memory or Intuition?

It can all sound so airy-fairy. And yet, haven't many of us held dreams of living in a world like this? Haven't we always had trouble ever understanding why wars happen, why people treat other people badly? Are these dreams of a just and peaceful world just magical thinking, something that could never actually happen?

Or are they perhaps memories of what we, thousands and thousands of years ago, once experienced—and at some point lost, as we descended into the kind of world we know of today filled with struggle, suffering and lack of direct connection with the Divine?

Or do these dreams perhaps come from intuitions about the future that is in store for us? Many of us are having these memories and intuitive feelings. Some of us feel we have been waiting thousands of years for these times we are now entering, times we knew would eventually be happening.

If we seek deeply within ourselves, we may find that these dreams of an ideal and peaceful world are actually both a distant memory of what we once experienced eons ago—and an intuitive glimpse into what is now again beginning to happen on Earth.

And our longing to return to this ideal world is simply a yearning to finally return to a Home we once knew.

If it all sounds too fantastical to be real, know that the reality of the Fifth Dimension is far beyond what the rational mind can grasp. See if you can move out of your mind and into a deeper aspect of your being to experience an intuitive knowing about it.

You may find that something in you deeply knows the reality of the Fifth Dimension, and that the return there is what you've been waiting to experience for a long, long time.

Exactly What are Dimensions?

Author and teacher Jim Self—an extraordinary man who humbly calls himself a "way shower"—has written books and articles about Ascension in which he explains very clearly his understanding of what dimensions are and how they differ from each other. Much of what follows in this chapter is a synopsis of how he explains them.

First of all, it's important to understand that dimensions are not places or locations; they're levels of consciousness that each vibrate at a certain rate. As we ascend, we will not be going anywhere. Much of what's around us will still be here. We will simply be perceiving and experiencing it all very differently, because our consciousness will be very different.

Each dimension vibrates at a higher rate than the one below. In each higher dimension, there exists a truer, broader perspective of reality, a greater level of knowing. We experience more freedom, greater power, and more opportunity to consciously create reality.

In order for a higher dimension to be available to us, we need to vibrate in resonance with it. Shifting from one level of consciousness to the next higher one means becoming established in the frequency of that consciousness, so we don't get pulled back.

During the process of Ascension, however, there are times when we can find ourselves shifting back and forth between dimensions, as we "visit" higher dimensions we will eventually be ascending into.

There exist numerous dimensions: the fourth and fifth are simply higher than the one we've been living in for thousands of years, known as the Third Dimension. Ascension into even higher dimensions will continue even after we've reached the Fifth. It's all part of the natural process of evolution.

The Third Dimension

It can be confusing to hear the term "third dimension". You might think this refers to the things you see: the table, the tree, the Earth. In this dimensional context, these things are seen as part of *form*—that which has shape, mass, texture and weight. Form is also present in the Fourth Dimension and to some degree in the Fifth. But in these higher dimensions, things are more light-filled, not as dense as they are in the Third.

According to certain sources, the planet and all that exists on it have actually left the Third Dimension; in fact, it no longer actually exists on the planet, having dissolved in December of 2012, when everything shifted into the Fourth Dimension.

However, most people have no idea this has happened or that a great deal more freedom is now available to them to create the lives they wish to live. It will take awhile before people give up operating from old habits they formed over thousands of years of living in the Third Dimension, believing in all the programmed restrictions and limitations of this lower dimension.

The Third Dimension is very familiar to us. Because we've been living in this reality for so many lifetimes, we tend to assume it is the only reality there is. We don't realize that it's only one very limited experience of reality that exists.

Third-Dimensional Beliefs

The third-dimensional "operating system" runs on rigid beliefs and a rather inflexible set of rules and limitations. For example, in the Third Dimension we learn to believe that physical bodies are solid; they can't walk through walls. They can only last a certain number of years; they're always susceptible to disease, they age and then they die.

Other third dimensional beliefs include the one that people are totally separate beings; we cannot merge with each other. We can only be in one place at a time. We can't read another person's mind. And once someone dies, we can no longer be in touch with them.

Duality

In third-dimensional consciousness, there is a solid belief in duality—up/down, big/small, etc. And often a belief that such opposites as good and bad, right and wrong, should and shouldn't all exist as absolutes. And because of this, judgment, blame, guilt, doubt, worry and fear are part of everyday existence.

The rational mind has been the instrument generally used to navigate through life in the Third Dimension. It's what has been used to make decisions and to decide what is real and what is not. In a way, the rational mind has been made "God" by most people in this dimension.

Third-Dimensional Time

Time in third-dimensional consciousness is fixed and linear—it only moves in a straight line in one direction, from past to present to future. This is seen as an absolute truth. There is no way to move back into the past or to change it. There's no way to be present now in the future.

All this, of course, is very familiar and is seen by most people on the planet to be the "truth" about reality. Whereas, in fact, it's only one state of consciousness that is available to us, especially now as we find ourselves in the Fourth Dimension.

The Fourth Dimension

As we become aware of the limiting constructs of the Third Dimension, we can begin to step out of our belief that we're still existing in it and move beyond its limits into the much freer atmosphere of the Fourth Dimension. This dimension has been open to us for a number of years; but it's not been till recently when the planet shifted into this dimension in 2012, that it's become totally and easily accessible to us.

The Earth and humanity will be traveling through this dimension for a relatively short period of time. This dimension can be seen as a "bridge" we are crossing, as we prepare ourselves for the Fifth. It's the dimension in which all the rapid transformation will be taking place.

There are many of us who are having more and more experiences of the Fourth Dimension, perhaps without realizing it. The most obvious sign that can indicate we're experiencing this new dimension is when we have experiences of spiritual awakening and heart opening.

Other times, we can be aware of it when we're simply feeling a sense of clarity and ease. Everything within and around us feels lighter, less rigid. There's a sense of spaciousness and upliftment—a greater freedom and feeling of empowerment. Everything feels more fluid—less static and fixed, and there's a knowing of endless possibility and a greater opportunity to change what is not working.

This is because, in the Fourth Dimension, we have greater access to the essence, power and wisdom of our Soul. As we begin to experience the frequencies of this higher presence flowing into our consciousness, we open to the higher aspects of ourselves and to abilities that allow us to understand reality on a deeper and broader scale.

Time in the Fourth Dimension

An interesting thing we can become aware of in the Fourth Dimension is that the experience of time is getting very strange. In particular, we may realize that time appears to be going faster and faster. There seems to be less and less time to get things done in our lives.

In reality, what's actually happening is that time is currently collapsing into the present moment, into the Now. It is no longer linear. In the Third Dimension, there was much focus on reacting to the past, and worrying or planning for the future. In the Fourth Dimension, we will be experiencing ourselves more and more in the present moment and simply living it.

The past will become a series of neutral experiences we merely use as reference points in speaking about events. The future will be something we can consciously plan for, without worry and without referencing the past.

If you think about it, you may realize that more and more, you have an ongoing sense of simply being in present time, with little interest—or even awareness—of past and future. It's easy to lose track altogether of time passing.

The Now is a very comfortable place to live in. Creative people have often naturally functioned from this aspect of fourth-dimensional consciousness, experiencing a space that could be called "no mind" in which awareness of time is absent—there is just the experience of Now, a space in which creation is happening.

Many athletes have also been familiar with this state of consciousness, when they've learned to gather all their awareness into the moment in order to perform optimally. And, of course, meditators for centuries have been familiar with this space of fourth-dimensional timelessness as well.

We can also discover in the Fourth Dimension that time is malleable—it can actually stretch and condense, much to our third-dimensional surprise. Think about it: have you had experiences lately in which time really has seemed to either stretch or condense itself—and you haven't been able to figure out what has happened?

With this shifting sense of time, we can also realize that manifestation is much faster than it was in the Third Dimension. If we're aware, we begin to see that we need to monitor our thoughts, or we will create things very quickly that we don't want in our lives. We have the opportunity to see quite clearly a concept we may have thought we understood before but are now experiencing first-hand: how we create our own reality.

Choice

In the Fourth Dimension, we can become aware that time is a point of power, in that each new moment is an opportunity for new beginnings and choices we can make.

We now have true choice in how to respond to life—something that did not exist in the Third Dimension. We can choose to step out of habits or reaction and restriction. We can choose to observe and make choices with clarity and awareness—without judgment or fear of punishment.

We can indeed choose or initiate something new in any given moment. In fact, what is true in one moment can be reversed in the next moment. This can give us an enormous power to change both how we respond to what is happening in our lives—and how it is actually happening.

For example, in the Third Dimension, you might have found yourself automatically reacting in anger over and over again to something someone said to you. You felt you had no control over your reaction—it would simply happen before you could do anything about it.

If you notice, you'll see that now in the Fourth Dimension, you have the freedom to pause first and choose your response. You can feel an emotion in one moment, and then choose to feel another one in the next. You can therefore have much more control over the outcome of situations you're in.

Thoughts in the Fourth Dimension

An interesting aspect of the Fourth Dimension is that it holds all thoughts that were ever thought by anyone in the Third Dimension. Thoughts don't just disappear—they continue to exist in the Fourth Dimension. All thoughts have a specific weight, texture, density and emotional charge. And they bond and cluster together with other similar thoughts in the same place through the principle of resonance.

There are many levels in the Fourth Dimension where thoughts gather, but they can generally be divided down into two major levels: the higher Fourth and the lower Fourth.

The lower Fourth Dimension is where all lower-vibrational thoughts, along with the emotions they create, cluster—such as fear, judgment, anger, blame, horror and guilt. All these thoughts are highly charged and heavy. People who have an abundance of these heavier thoughts and emotions have generally moved into these lower levels of the Fourth Dimension since the Shift of the Earth in December 2012.

Likewise, all people who resonate with the more positive thoughts and emotions found in the higher Fourth Dimension have found themselves shifting into this level of this dimension. Therefore, as time goes on, you may be finding yourself more and more around people who are vibrating at a frequency similar to your own.

Those of us living primarily on this level of the Fourth Dimension are becoming aware that there's a sense of natural well-being that becomes more and more available to us. We can feel lighter, more joyful and free than before. We can more easily experience deep inner peace, love and gratitude.

The "rules" of the higher Fourth Dimension provide a greater sense of ease, possibility and capability. We have an ability to access greater power to create what we need and want. We also have a wider view of reality which brings in a calmer, quieter sense of being. We feel more detached, less reactive to life around us. We can often feel a sense of being filled with light.

The Fifth Dimension

The Fifth Dimension has often been described as the dimension of love, of living totally from the Heart. It's where we will finally awaken into full consciousness of who we are and live in the true knowing of the oneness of all that exists.

It's a dimension of no limitations in which all possibilities are available. Physical density is gone. Form is fluid and the structure of physical bodies has turned to Light.

In this dimension, we will merge and reintegrate with our Soul. We will begin to experience who we actually are—truly powerful multi-dimensional beings. Our full DNA will be activated and the 90% of our brain that's been dormant for thousands of years will come alive again.

As fifth-dimensional beings, we will live in ongoing resonance with such feelings as love, joy, enthusiasm, beauty, kindness and reverence. Cooperation, co-creation, and collaboration will come naturally to us as we work and create together.

We will experience psychic abilities we once had long ago, such as telepathy and clairvoyance. Much of what we will experience will pour forth wordlessly from our Hearts, rather than from our minds. Speaking will not be necessary.

As conscious beings, we will be able to access within ourselves information and wisdom that resides in all dimensions. We will experience a oneness with all that is, with no sense of separation. We will think from our Hearts and make soul-guided choices.

We Can't Take Our Baggage with Us

What's important to understand is that in order to live in the Fifth Dimension where this high vibration exists, all mental and emotional baggage we carry must be left at the door. No fear, anger, hostility, sadness, guilt exists there—no suffering or sense of separation. These emotions and thoughts are all based on the illusion of separation that exists only in the Third and Fourth Dimensions.

As you can imagine, in order to be able to achieve this kind of clarity and shift permanently into the Fifth Dimension, most of us need to do a great amount of clearing of negative and limiting emotions, thoughts and patterns that we carry not only from this lifetime, but from many other lifetimes we've lived. It will be a process that will probably stretch over a number of years.

The Fifth Dimension operates very differently from the Fourth. On some of the higher levels, there is no need to eat, drink or sleep. There's no need to be concerned about clothing ourselves or finding shelter. There is no aging, no death (unless chosen)—and we can change what we'd like about our bodies. The whole notion of having to survive through "the sweat of your brow" is non-existent.

Time in the Fifth Dimension

Time in the Fifth Dimension is even more fluid than in the Fourth. Some describe it as "simultaneous time" or "everything happening at once." You can see all past and future lifetimes simultaneously. You can see all timelines available, all possibilities.

Cycles of day and night still exist, but they're just seen as mechanical markers. They have no effect on the Now that is happening. Perhaps you are already having flashes of this experience of time and haven't been able to put words to it.

Manifestation in the Fifth Dimension is instantaneous: you focus on something in your mind—it appears. In one way, we had a kind of advantage living in the Third Dimension in that there was a time buffer between what we thought and what we manifested. It gave us room to practice honing our manifestation skills.

However, most of us during our long passage through the Third Dimension were sloppy with that time buffer, as we didn't understand what it was. We didn't comprehend how we were creating our future reality with our current thoughts and emotions. We thought and felt anything we wanted to, believing there'd be no problem since we couldn't see the results instantaneously.

This is no longer true now that we're in the Fourth Dimension. Our thoughts are manifesting our future much more quickly now. If you can notice this, you can practice becoming master of your thoughts—one of the requisites to live in the Fifth Dimension.

Space in the Fifth Dimension

The experience of space in the Fifth Dimension is also quite different from that in the Fourth. You can simply think of a place, and you find yourself there.

There's also a type of merging that can take place, causing a very different kind of experience when two objects or people come together. For example, in the Third and Fourth Dimensions, if your car hits a tree, both are generally damaged. In the Fifth Dimension, the molecules of the car, you, and the tree simply merge for a bit, then separate again. No damage is done—you've just experienced a moment of unity with both the car and the tree.

When you encounter another being in the Fifth Dimension you can also experience a type of merging with them when you come together. This is a blissful feeling of actually becoming one unified organism for a bit, in which the molecules of both of you intermingle. This particular type of union is non-existent on lower dimensions.

No Secrets

There are no secrets in the Fifth Dimension—everyone is transparent. People generally communicate through telepathy and have the ability to read each other's thoughts and feelings with ease. Because of this, there's no possibility of hiding anything. But then, the good news is there is no need for secrets!

All this may seem like a type of fantasy land. But many of us are already having experiences or dreams that feel like visits to the Fifth Dimension.

These experiences are exhilarating—tremendously exciting and hopeful. They keep us moving on through the difficulties that sometimes arise as we travel through the rapid changes in the Fourth Dimension and into the Fifth. And they give us the experience of knowing that Ascension into a higher reality is really happening.

When Will Ascension be Complete?

Some sources say this Shift that the Earth and humanity are making into the Fifth Dimension will probably be complete within the next decade or so; others give no date. But all seem to agree it will be sometime in the near future, although many individuals will be moving into the Fifth Dimension at their own rate sooner when their frequency is high enough to match the vibration of this higher dimension.

You might ask: How can this possibly happen so quickly? How can this world turn around from where it is today and become this utopian kind of world? There is still so much darkness on the planet—wars, hatred, prejudice and injustice.

The answer is two-fold: First, thousands of people on the planet are now already experiencing awakening at an unprecedented rate—and this awakening appears to be accelerating as time goes by. At some point, the hundredth monkey phenomenon will inevitably take hold.

And secondly, not everyone on the planet at this time is making the choice (consciously or unconsciously) to make the shift into the Fifth Dimension.

All Souls on the Earth have the choice to enter this new dimension, given they have assimilated sufficient light to hold the frequency that exists in that higher dimension. But many will be choosing to leave the Earth within the next decade or so to move on to other third-dimensional experiences in other parts of the universe because they will not have finished with what their Higher Selves wish to experience in third-dimensional reality.

Those of us who are choosing to stay and make the shift with the Earth may be going through some intense and rapid changes, as our bodies and minds make the radical shifts needed to move into the higher consciousness requisite for moving into the Fifth Dimension.

Chapter 3
The Fall of Consciousness

In your innermost being, you may experience a keen resonance with the Fifth Dimension and feel that you at one time actually existed there. Because it is so familiar, a sense of poignant longing may arise in you to return there.

Many of us feel this way. And it's because we have a memory (either conscious or unconscious) of what we once knew long ago, before what is known as the "Fall of Consciousness" took place.

At one time, according to a number of sources, the Earth and all beings on it were living in the Fifth Dimension. At some point, many of us decided that we wanted to experience something new—something that had been recently created in the universe: the Fourth Dimension. This was a consciousness that was denser than what anyone had ever experienced before in the universe and had never been explored before.

In this new dimension, there existed a number of what could be called "mutations" or distortions of Truth. In the higher dimensions, only vibrations of love, peace and harmony existed. In this new dimension, certain denser vibrations such as hatred, sorrow, guilt, shame, anger, and distortions of power had also come into existence.

We were given free will to go into this dimension and explore these new distorted vibrations—and also to experience cause and effect and the results of our choices and actions. It was an adventure, something new to experience.

At some point, our explorations took us down deeper into even denser experiences into a realm known as the Third Dimension, which had also recently come into being. Here it really became an adventure because it was very dark and seemingly cut off from the rest of the higher dimensions, as well as from other worlds and galactic races we'd known. This is where we really began experiencing the Fall of Consciousness.

We Chose the Mission

But what's important to understand is that the Fall of Consciousness doesn't necessarily refer to a mistake that happened, or that those of us who volunteered to go on this exploratory mission were souls who "fell out of Grace". This was an interpretation devised much later after the Fall of Consciousness had happened by forces wanting to keep humanity disempowered.

In actuality, we chose the mission. We had been asked if we would go and fully experience all the mutations and distortions—and then to eventually bring them back Home to be cleared from the universe. And we volunteered to do this.

What we didn't realize in signing up for this exploration was the extent to which we'd be experiencing the density of this dimension. We didn't know we would become so immersed in the negative frequencies that existed here that we'd forget who we were and where we came from.

We didn't know we'd lose the direct connection to the Divine we'd always known or that our internal guidance system would essentially be closed down. We didn't understand that we'd only have 10% of our brain available to us, or that we'd lose most of our spiritual abilities we'd always been able to rely upon. And we didn't understand how difficult it would be to encounter energies we'd never before experienced, such as fear, judgment, separation and enslavement.

But all this did happen, and it's therefore been extremely challenging—to say the least!—to explore and experience this Third Dimension.

You may have memories arising of lifetimes you spent in the last days of Atlantis, when it was clear that the Fall of Consciousness into the lower dimensions was beginning to happen—and that the vibrations of the Fifth Dimension were slipping away. You may now be re-experiencing the trauma and anguish many felt during those times, knowing what was happening. Even though you'd chosen to be part of that drama, you were now frightened of what this choice actually entailed.

Know that if you're having these kinds of memories, now is the time to release them. Re-experience briefly any pain that may come up with them—but then let them go. Don't dwell on them or romanticize them. It's time to be finished with this whole exploration into those lower dimensions.

It's Time to Return Home

The incredible news is that this exploration is finally over. We have learned all we're going to from this third-dimensional experience. And it's time for us to remember who we are. It's time for us finally to return Home.

Feel into the joy of this! This long experience you've had exploring the realms of suffering is actually coming to a close. And you don't have to do a whole lot to make this happen. Ascension is simply happening and you're coming with it.

It is said that those of us who have spent these thousands of years exploring and experiencing the Third Dimension are seen as magnificent and powerful Souls by inhabitants of other planets and star systems who are now watching us move through this Ascension process with keen interest. They see us as enormously courageous Souls and hold great respect and love for us.

The Death of a Myth

Although it has not been easy to do what we've done, most of us all during our lifetimes in the Third Dimension have believed a powerful myth that thrived in that dimension. This is the myth that there is something inherently wrong with us; we are creatures who have been born into sin—or we're here to pay back our bad karma—or however it's framed. We are inherently bad and have cause to feel shame about who we are.

Most of us have believed this myth lifetime after lifetime and have followed teachings that say we need to learn how to be good and to constantly improve ourselves. If we don't, we will be punished in some way. Because of the belief in this myth, many people have been easily subjugated and controlled through religions, elite groups, and educational systems throughout history.

This myth is now being exposed in many ways across the planet. People are waking up to the Truth of who they are and what they deserve and to the lies they've been programmed with. And, as you move more and more into fourth-dimensional awareness, you will see this myth begin to disintegrate in your own personal life, as well as in the collective.

The Light of who you actually are, a courageous Soul who took on a mission where few others would venture, will begin to shine through into your awareness more and more. And the deep (and often unconscious) shame for being a human being who's bumbled around in the dark for lifetimes, making one "mistake" after another, will wash away.

It's Up to Each of Us

Ascension is happening. We are all experiencing it whether we're aware of it yet or not. It's important to understand that there is no "right" way to experience it. There's only the way we choose to experience it.

One choice is to simply allow life to transform you—because it will. Sometimes in uncomfortable ways, especially if you have any resistance to change. But rest assured, if you've chosen to ascend, life will do the job for you.

Another choice is to consciously and actively cooperate with the shifts taking place inside you. You can become what's been called a "conscious evolutionary." You can willingly let go of old third-dimensional patterns, release negative emotions, judgments and thoughts, and work on keeping your vibration high as much as possible.

These efforts will likely ensure that your journey through the Fourth Dimension will be a lot smoother and even perhaps more rapid.

In the rest of this book, we will be looking specifically at how Ascension may be manifesting in your personal life—and what you can do to help make this journey a smoother, easier one—and if possible, one filled with joy, upliftment and radiant beauty.

There are no two ways about it—this is an extraordinary journey you've signed up for. No one said it was going to be easy. But when you ponder for a moment where it is you're traveling to, it's hard to feel anything but relief and profound joy that it's happening.

Understanding the
Ascension Process

Chapter 4
The Experience of Ascension

So what does this dimensional shift mean for us on the personal level? It's of course somewhat different for each of us, but there are some common experiences that many of us who are entering deeply into the process of Ascension seem to be having.

In general, there can be the experience of no longer feeling like we're standing on solid ground—shifting sands are appearing everywhere under our feet. It's as if we're standing in two worlds at once, functioning in both the familiar Third Dimension and also in the new energies of the Fourth and Fifth. At times, we feel like we're experiencing enormous energetic shifts that leave us reeling.

Another way to describe it might be that a marriage between spirit and matter seems to be taking place. We're beginning to integrate with our Souls, and we're becoming more light-embodied human beings.

Profound Transformational Process

Have no doubt about it—Ascension is a profound transformational process. We are leaving behind a way of life we have been living for thousands of years. We're being called to let go of an entire set of beliefs about who we are, what life is, and what reality is.

The waves of Light now flooding the earth are beginning to wash away all memories, thoughts, emotions, and beliefs that aren't aligned with the new fifth-dimensional consciousness we're growing into.

As described in Chapter One, this process can bring about some intense and unsettling experiences. A sense of disorientation can occur, along with the revisiting of old, heavy emotions and memories that arise seemingly out of nowhere—emotions we've thought we left far behind.

Unresolved conflicts from the past may also surface, demanding attention. Certain beliefs we've had forever no longer make sense; assumptions we've had about our-selves, life and reality are proving to be false; interests and passions we've held for a long time are beginning to fade.

At times, we may wonder who we actually are—because we are becoming unfamiliar even to ourselves. In fact, we may no longer be able to predict anything accu-rately about ourselves or about what will probably hap-pen in our life.

In short, we may feel we're on a roller coaster that both revisits our past and brings us into uncharted terri-tory without reference points. It feels foreign and unset-tling. Everything feels like it's shifting—because it *is*. We are rapidly moving into a dimension in which reality is very different from what we've been used to in the Third and Fourth Dimensions.

Spiritual Deepening

At times, it can feel like a crazy paradoxical experience. On the one hand, moments of spiritual awakening may be happening more frequently, bringing a sense of deepening into a more profound aspect of our being.

We might realize that in one way, we're feeling a great-er sense of expansive joy in our everyday life, sometimes at surprising times when we'd think we should actually be feeling unhappy. And maybe we find ourselves having positive expectations about something that might sound crazy to other people. We realize that our trust in the divine plan of our life gives us an ability to simply trust and go with the flow more often.

We also occasionally have "love attacks" that descend on us out of nowhere, in which love for someone, even everyone and everything, floods our whole being—causing our chest to expand, leaving us unable to speak.

At times, we find that we have greater inner strength than we could ever imagine, as well as an unlimited capacity to forgive. We experience enormous ongoing gratitude, even for the smallest things. And beauty, which seems to be showing up everywhere, occasionally touches us so profoundly, we're reduced to tears.

We might also sometimes become more aware of the presence of guides and other beings around us, giving us support—and a deeper connection with our own divinity. And, much to our delight, we are discovering a greater ability within us to create magic and synchronicity in our lives.

In fact, all the higher fourth and fifth-dimensional energies seem to now be more available to us—love, peace, freedom, ease and joy can all come present if we stop to look for them within us. We can simply focus on them, and they begin to flow through our entire being.

Old Energies Leaving

On the other hand, paradoxically, we can also experience at times a lot of pain and confusion, as old, dense energies and dysfunctional patterns arise to be released. In the process, we may experience emotions we haven't felt for a long time, such as depression, despair, fear and anxiety.

Indeed, one thing that can probably be said with certainty is that during this time of Ascension, all our "stuff" is going to be coming up—relationship stuff, money stuff, health stuff, job stuff, identity stuff. Everything that we are *not* will be shown to us, so it can be left behind.

What's interesting is how both the joyful, uplifting experiences and the challenging, unhappy ones can arise and fade very quickly and follow one upon the other. Even the most emotionally-steady among us may swing from a mood of cheerful optimism—to an experience of intense pain and confusion—to a feeling of exhilarating joy—all in one day. And sometimes all even at the same time.

New Openings

Another phenomenon we can experience during the process of Ascension is a sense that our brain is being "rewired". We may feel strange energies running through our head from time to time—sometimes a sense of pressure or on and off pain in different parts of our head. Strange memory lapses may occur.

It can feel like "doors" are being opened up in our brain in that we've now got access to a new kind of intelligence, a new wisdom. A deep and expanded knowing just somehow shows up in us, offering us new perceptions of the world and how reality works. We are opening to the wisdom of our true self.

It's like we're waking up from a long sleep of forgetfulness. In reality, none of the "new" wisdom we're waking up to is actually new. We've known it all before; we are simply remembering it. It may include remembering past lifetimes or seeing the big picture of the true history of humanity's existence on Earth. We may begin to understand things about humanity and the cosmos we've never understood before.

We may also discover that out of nowhere, we suddenly seem to have new tools and psychic abilities we haven't had before. New information is now within our memory that wasn't there before—realizations of our spiritual heritage, memories of other planets we've existed on, other galaxies we've visited. And our ability to "see" into other people and know what they're feeling is expanding.

Sometimes it seems as if we're actually feeling the solar activity that's currently flooding the planet. Or that we feel events that are occurring on the other side of the planet. We suddenly feel in tune with whole groups of people in the world we've never met before.

All of these new openings and skills, although indisputably exciting, can be challenging at times, especially as we attempt to go about our life in our old familiar ways, working at jobs and functioning within relationships. The sense of disorientation can make us feel unreal, ungrounded, and even dysfunctional at times.

In some ways, you may think that all these kinds of changes can sound a lot like what has already been happening in your life since you started on a conscious path of awakening. And they are.

The big difference is the pace at which it will all continue to happen. At times, you may feel as if you're barely taking a breath after your last releasing of old emotions or new opening, and the next challenging experience appears. Also the intensity of these inner experiences will likely be greater for you than what you've experienced till now on your path of awareness.

In the following chapters, we will look at some of the specific experiences and challenges you may face during your process of Ascension and offer suggestions about how to meet them with as much grace and ease as possible.

Some of the "symptoms" described may sound familiar to you. And some of them difficult or unpleasant. If you can learn to trust and surrender to what is happening, your passage through these shifts can actually be swift and even exciting.

Indeed, you may feel much joy as you experience yourself being carried along on the waves of expansion into new realities you've never known before. Even when you're in the middle of uncomfortable shifts in your life, you can remember the bigger picture of what is actually happening and experience the excitement of this. And you can rejoice as you witness old emotional baggage falling away, sometimes effortlessly.

Chapter 5
Ascension Body Symptoms

A major symptom that appears to be part of the Ascension process is feeling puzzling, unexplainable changes in the body. This makes sense, as our bodies, of course, need to change along with the rest of us.

In fact, every aspect of our physical bodies is undergoing a dynamic metamorphosis, in every cell. All systems in our bodies are changing. Dormant genes are being activated in our DNA, causing new and unfamiliar chemical changes. Our bodies are shifting from carbon-based organisms to crystalline "light bodies".

And if, on top of this, we're also moving rapidly through a lot of mental, emotional and spiritual changes, our bodies may really be struggling at times to keep up.

Aches & Pains

For instance, you may find yourself with unusual body aches and pains—some that seem to appear and disappear, others that jump around to different parts of your body. Headaches that come and go can be a common experience.

Old injuries you thought were healed long ago may begin showing up again. Or you might feel waves of heat or energy passing through your body at odd times. Flu-like symptoms may also come and go. Because these symptoms are so common in people experiencing Ascension, they've been referred to as the "Ascension flu".

Changes in Sleep Patterns

Something else that is being reported during these times is a change taking place in people's sleep patterns. You may find that suddenly you seem to need a whole lot more sleep than usual. You may at times wake up feeling drugged and have a sense that you've "been somewhere" and "done a lot" in the sleep state, although you can't remember what.

You may go through periods of time in which you find yourself having intense dreams every night. You may find monsters and battles appearing in these dreams or other fearful kinds of scenarios. Don't be concerned with these—they're simply signs that old, negative patterns and memories are releasing.

You may also find that at times during the day, your whole body suddenly pulls on you, demanding a nap. You're afraid to close your eyes, because you know you'll immediately fall asleep if you do. It's important when this happens to give in to these nap attacks if you can.

Usually they're short—maybe 15 to 20 minutes. But when you feel the pull to sleep, know that there's something that wants to happen that would be best to happen at that point in time, and the process requires that you be totally still and asleep.

If you can't conveniently take a nap when this happens, don't worry. What needs to happen will just wait until you're asleep at night. It's just that the particular time you're feeling pulled into sleep would be the best time for whatever needs to occur, if it's possible for you to take that time to fall asleep.

There are other times when you may go through periods in which you find you get along on a lot *less* sleep than normal. You may actually find yourself waking up every night for a while, often between 2 and 4 am, not knowing why you can't sleep. Again, don't be concerned. And don't fret about missing out on your sleep.

Use this time to meditate (sometimes the best time to do this anyway) or quietly read. Trust that when you wake up later in the morning, you will feel rested and able to move into your day with ease—and you surprisingly will be able to. There are natural and essential processes occurring here that can't be explained or understood by the medical or scientific communities, nor by the rational mind.

Exhaustion

Yet another common Ascension symptom is utter exhaustion. This may happen on and off for a while. It actually shouldn't be a surprise to feel exhausted at times during this Ascension process, since so much is happening in the body-mind.

If you're feeling a constant swing between your old third-dimensional consciousness and your new fourth-dimensional consciousness, it's natural that this might wear you out. Constant change can cause stress on your body.

Sometimes it can be especially difficult if you're around people who seem to be totally "asleep" to what's happening and they're functioning in low third-dimensional types of energies, caught in anger, depression, or other heavy emotions. It's sometimes hard to hold your own vibration when you're feeling assaulted by negativity from other people or you're in the presence of a lot of unconsciousness.

Of course, some of the negativity that's exhausting you might be your own! But don't get down on yourself if this happens. The emotions you're experiencing are coming up to be released—it's all part of the Ascension process. Just realize that you need to be kind to yourself if you feel deep fatigue after experiencing a lot of releasing, either from other people or from within yourself.

Sometimes exhaustion sets in simply because your body is having to adjust to new, higher frequencies. Remember, you're in the process of being completely rewired—your body is morphing into a much less dense light-body. It's busy absorbing new energies and transforming itself—it's shedding old energies, rebooting itself, disassembling and reconstructing itself. Deep changes on the DNA level are taking place. Your whole system is adapting to a brand new "operating system". It's no wonder if you feel exhausted!

Try to give your body all the rest and sleep it needs. Be kind to it. It will eventually adjust to the new levels of consciousness you're ascending to and you'll feel more energy again.

Is it Ascension or Something to be Concerned About?

Of course, it's very important to always check body symptoms out with a health professional, especially if they feel serious and they're ongoing. Don't take chances with your health.

But if the person you go to can't figure out why you're experiencing the symptoms you are, or they assure you they're not something you need to worry about, it's likely the symptoms are connected to your Ascension process.

But then, your symptoms may be both: they may have been brought about by the Ascension process AND they possibly could be helped by medical attention. So check out anything that persists to cause you discomfort.

What seems important during these times is that you take especially good care of your body. You may well be someone who has chosen on the Soul level to take your body with you into the Fifth Dimension. (Many people will be doing this.) So you'll want to keep it in as good health as possible to make this transition an easier one.

Also remember that with all the changes happening to your body, it's a lot more sensitive and vulnerable than it used to be. In fact, you may be experiencing hypersensitivity to certain things you never have before, such as specific smells, loud noises, particular foods or bright lights. You may have trouble listening to a number of people speaking at once in a room.

It's as if your nervous system goes on overload with any of these things. This may be par for the course in your Ascension process. So just take care of yourself and avoid these kinds of unpleasant experiences if you can.

Remember that your body needs a great deal of loving care. In particular, pay close attention to keeping your immune system as strong as possible. You can do this with health supplements, exercise and diet—and drinking lots of water.

You can also take advantage of the many new energy healing methods appearing on the planet—such as sound healing, color therapy, and light therapy. Of course, there are also practices that have been around for awhile, such as Reiki and other hands-on healing methods, as well as subtle energy approaches such as flower essences, homeopathy and essential oils that can be equally helpful.

As we move more deeply into the Fourth Dimension, these types of energetic healing methods will become more and more popular, as they're designed to heal on a more subtle level than traditional types of healing methods—something more and more people will be resonating with.

Watch your Thoughts and Emotions

It's also important to understand that your negative thoughts and emotions may also bring about illness. The next time you catch a cold or flu, look back at what you were going through emotionally right before you began coming down with the symptoms, and you may be able to see how your emotions and the onset of your symptoms are connected.

Negative emotions lower our vibration. And it's when we're in a lower vibration that we are susceptible to bacteria and viruses that also vibrate at that same level. One of the best preventive measures we can take when it comes to colds and flus is to keep our vibration high. (Suggestions for doing this appear in Chapters 11 and 12.)

Of course, this may be difficult to do on a constant basis, given the challenges that Ascension brings and all that shows up in the course of your life during this accelerating time—so be gentle with yourself.

Allow your body to cleanse itself of whatever toxins it's dealing with. Actually, colds and flus can simply be seen as cleansings—they're uncomfortable, but they're the way our bodies deal with toxins, both physical and emotional.

Changes in Your Diet

You may find at some point that your body is no longer attracted to certain foods and spices, even those you've loved for years. It's important to follow your body's lead in this matter. Tune into what it's telling you it needs.

As you go through the Ascension process, your body needs particular foods to assist it as it shifts to a new frequency. Be careful of the tendency to think that you know better than your body about what you should be eating, simply because of something you've read or have always understood to be healthy. Your body knows best and will communicate its needs to you, if you listen to it.

These are particular times happening now—old, general rules about diet may no longer apply to your body. It's probable that the old standby guidelines, such as staying away from sugar, chocolate, caffeine and intoxicants, are still applicable. And you probably can't go wrong with eating a lot of fresh vegetables.

But check it out with your own body—it is unique and it's going through its own unique changes. You may be developing sensitivities to certain foods you never had before, such as gluten and dairy products. If you find you are, perhaps you can give these foods up for a while to see if your body feels better.

And stay tuned: changes might continue to happen. Don't assume a particular change is going to last forever. Stay in communication with your body on an on-going basis.

A difficulty can arise, however, when you feel you're getting different messages from different parts of your body. Your tongue may be telling you one thing: for example, that it wants sweets or salty, starchy foods. Unfortunately, the tongue seems to focus on immediate pleasure and not on what might be best for the body.

It's better to try to listen to your stomach or your digestive system. These will probably give you better information as to what your body really needs.

Some people hear their bodies speaking, others receive messages through feeling or simply knowing. Still others get actual body sensations, such as a feeling of nausea in just thinking about eating something. Or a feeling of body relaxation or an energy lift. Find out how your particular body wants to communicate with you.

Your Body Needs your Love

The main thing to remember with all these body changes is that what your body needs above everything else is your love. In particular, if it's not feeling well, try sending love to your cells and your organs rather than anger, demands or impatience.

Spend time doing this by actually feeling and seeing your love entering your cells. It can be amazing to see how pain can diminish and even cease when you do this with true compassion and concern.

Really appreciate your body—especially for how it has put up with your taking it for granted your whole life. If you're like most people you probably don't often stop to consider the fact, for instance, that your heart continues to pump blood 24/7. Or that your digestive system continues to take in whatever you feed it and does its darnedest to digest it one way or another. And your lungs continue to take in oxygen and your blood circulates it throughout your body. Everything your body does is actually miraculous. Take time to acknowledge this miracle.

Become aware also of any judgments you may have about how your body looks. Your body feels these. If you can't change your judgments, then at least express an apology to your body for having them. Your body is doing its best to be the best body for you it can. If you can at least give it appreciation and send it love and gratitude regularly, you'll see how eagerly it responds to this kind of caring attention.

Consider that your body can be seen as a servant who has worked for you your entire life. It's been on duty doing its job continuously, providing you with a physical vehicle so that you, as a Soul, can function here on this physical plane. It's been a very devoted and willing servant; it has done everything it can to keep providing you with a dependable means to live and act in the world.

Tune into yourself for a moment: How good an employer have you been? How compassionate have you been to this devoted servant? How do you meet its needs? How well have you shown your appreciation for its devotion--especially during these stressful times of Ascension, when so much is being released from your body and so much Light is pushing its way into your cells?

If you find this process of body transformation challenging at times, remember that this body "upgrade" is connecting you more fully to your divine multidimensional self; it's giving you greater access to your Soul. All physical and emotional toxins must be cleared out of your cells before more light may enter them.

Remember to ask for divine support. Envision the transformation happening with ease and grace. Welcome the changes, inviting more conscious light energy into your cells—and especially into all the places where you hold pain or tension. You'll find that your body hungers for this light.

Chapter 6
Disorientation

A sense of disorientation from time to time also seems to be part of the Ascension process. Perhaps you're noticing a sensation of not feeling grounded in what you've known to be your usual, familiar "self"—both physically and psychologically. Or maybe you have a sense that the world around you somehow isn't as "real" as it used to be.

It can also be a feeling of being in limbo: you're floating between an older identity you've had for a long time and an unfamiliar one that seems to be moving in. So much of what used to be comfortable doesn't fit or feel right anymore. All your old reference points are disappearing.

Or you might describe it as a sense of walking between two worlds, neither of which you're fully in. You know that you're not "all here"—and yet you don't know where the rest of you is.

All this can be disconcerting, and at times even a little scary.

Physical Disorientation

Sometimes you may feel ungrounded and dizzy, or even spatially-challenged. You might find yourself knocking against the side of a doorway as you walk through it or actually walking into a wall. Perhaps you go to put a cup on a counter and find that you've missed the edge by a couple of inches and the cup drops to the floor. You've never been clumsy before, but here you are not being able to judge physical distances accurately.

All this is totally normal when experiencing a wave of Ascension: the fact is you're *not* all here. You're living in two different dimensions at once. You're in transition into a whole new realm of reality, and your body can sometimes lag behind in another reality.

Psychological Disorientation

This sense of living in two realities at once may also create strange psychological experiences. It's natural to feel somewhat disoriented if you're generally living in a high frequency of love and non-separation—and yet you're still engaged in old third-dimensional activities and relationships based in separation and limitation. It's as if the two realities collide inside you and you can't tell what is real anymore.

At times, you may have the feeling of living in a bubble, feeling separate from the outside world and knowing no way to get out of it. Or you may have a sensation of directing your life by remote control.

On top of all that, you may also be experiencing periods of brainfog in which your mind is fuzzy and your cognitive abilities seem impaired. At times you can't recall names of familiar people, books or movies—or even simple, familiar words like "tree" or "foot".

You might think you're experiencing dementia as your memory seems to be disappearing. Of course, it could be a sign of aging; if you're concerned, you might want to check it out with a health practitioner.

But it may well also be part of the Ascension process. The waves of light flooding the planet are causing the release of memories, especially the ones with negative charges attached to them. And simple words can temporarily get swept away by these waves because they're attached to the dysfunctional patterns being released.

All this can be very disconcerting if you don't keep in mind that disorientation is to be expected as you traverse the unfamiliar terrain between the Third and Fifth Dimensions. And if you watch, you'll notice the words always do come back to you eventually.

Focus on the New Coming In

If you can keep in mind that all these experiences of disorientation are part of the Ascension process—the old is leaving and the new is coming in—it can be easier to handle the discomforts of the transition. And, more importantly, if you can focus your attention on the "new you" and the "new life" you're beginning to experience, rather than on what is leaving, it will be a lot more enjoyable and uplifting. You can help to ground the new energies inside you this way and begin to experience them more fully.

Release and opening always go hand in hand. Rather than trying to hold on to what is leaving, focus on what new reality may be opening up inside of you. You may be surprised to find that what you've always wished for is finally appearing. And the new life beginning to manifest is much more beautiful and fulfilling than you ever dreamed possible.

Embracing the Unknown

You may find that the further you travel into the Fourth Dimension, the more you are being compelled to walk into the mysterious depths of the Unknown. You're being called to move forward without knowing where you are going or what awaits you when you get there. Know that this is a necessary passage.

Loss May be Necessary

In the process, you may also be experiencing unwelcome losses. Remember that in your Ascension process, letting go of familiar third-dimensional thoughts, beliefs, feelings and perceptions of reality you've been living with is necessary. You need to leave them behind. They are too limited and are based in fear and programmed perceptions of separation.

You may also find that you're being compelled to leave behind familiar relationships or a job which no longer support your evolving consciousness. Or you may find you need to move to a new home in an unfamiliar community.

With these kinds of changes, everything can feel uncomfortable and uncertain. If you look into the future, you may not see anything familiar—or maybe even anything at all. It looks blank, empty, unpredictable and even "unsafe".

You'll find that it's necessary to learn to be comfortable with the Unknown, because you really have no choice. You can't take your baggage with you. Anything that is not based in truth, that does not support the essential *you*, must be left behind.

You are Not Alone

Walking into the Unknown takes great trust and courage. Although it may feel frightening and at times that you're alone on your journey, know that your Higher Self is always there with you, guiding you perfectly. It knows what you can take with you and what you need to leave behind. It is preparing you for your transition into a higher vibration in the very best way for you.

Indeed, what if you were to become aware that the loss or difficult situations you are experiencing are actually expressions of great love of that Higher You that is guiding you? Feel into that possibility and see if something shifts inside of you.

Know too that your guides are also always with you—as well as many other beings in the invisible realms wanting to assist you, if you simply ask them. Even if you can't see or hear them, know they are there. See what starts happening in your life with their help when you ask for it. What you can begin discovering is that you have much help available to you in the invisible realms. Indeed, you can discover that you are greatly loved.

The Unknown need not be scary. It can be experienced as an exciting adventure. Be willing to let go of all familiar, comfortable ways in which you've been living and see what happens. Ask yourself: Who am I becoming? What will my life look like? And see what shows up.

Experience of Being Multi-Dimensional

Part of the Ascension process is becoming aware that you are a multi-dimensional being. As time goes on, you'll likely realize that there is much, much more of you than you've been aware of.

The little human form you may take yourself to be is only one small aspect of who you are. In reality, you are a magnificent, powerful being existing in multiple locations, dimensions and timelines.

It may be a bit much to take in at this point, but you will likely come to recognize the times when this multi-layered reality of who you are begins to seep into your awareness.

For instance, you may find yourself at some point thinking of more than one thing at a time, as if you have more than one brain at work. Or you may respond to something in two or three different ways simultaneous-ly—sometimes in opposition to each other. You can get to feel like a split personality.

Another version of this is experiencing something in two different time frames simultaneously. Or experiencing yourself to be in two different places. These are all experiences of moving into higher fourth-dimensional awareness. You start realizing that both time and space are fluid, not at all static.

Extraterrestrial Heritage

A number of people are waking up to the knowledge of their extraterrestrial heritage. They are remembering who they were before coming into this lifetime—or who they were before they first came to Earth and incarnated as a human being thousands of years ago.

Some know they were originally Pleiadian, others Sirian or Arcturian. Some are from star systems most of us have never heard of. And some are remembering this heritage clearly, along with lifetimes they had as these beings in ancient times on Earth in Lemuria or Atlantis.

For those having these experiences, this is more than just romantic daydreaming or a desire for a more exciting identity. The memory and knowing are very real. And as they step more fully into these identities, things that have been puzzling about their lives and how they've lived them start to finally make sense.

If this kind of realization comes to you at some point, know that it can be disorienting at first. But it can ultimately help you to finally discover what has been so different about you your whole life, compared to many of the "earthlings" here.

You can at last settle into your unique differentness without feeling there's something wrong with you. You can appreciate very clearly what it's like to be a Harry Potter living among Muggles.

The discovery of your galactic heritage may also help you to begin remembering extraordinary skills and abilities you naturally had at one point long ago that you can now begin to remember and use.

What may take a while is adjusting to the sensation of being more than one identity. You are in fact human, here in this body. And on some other level or dimension, you may also be a being that is living somewhere else or in a parallel reality. Remember, in the Fifth Dimension, you become aware of all your lifetimes occurring simultaneously. This may be what you're tapping into.

This can all sound and feel crazy at first. You may feel you're having an identity crisis. But you just need to let go of the belief that most or all of your being exists here and now with this physical body and is run by your rational mind. Because this simply isn't true. You are much, much more than this.

Ground Yourself

If you are feeling disoriented due to any of the above-described experiences, it may be important for you to take time to ground yourself on a daily basis. Understand that your brain is undergoing profound and radical changes, as the high frequencies streaming onto the Earth work to shift and open up new awareness and memories within you. This is part of your rewiring and recalibration.

At one time, your brain was functioning at a much higher level than it is now, back in the times of Lemuria or the early Atlantian days before the Fall of Consciousness and spiritual darkness descended onto the Earth. It is time now for your brain to open up again to those higher functions you once had.

But this rewiring and restructuring of your brain can cause you to feel ungrounded. And when you feel it happening, it might be important to ground yourself in the Earth's energy. The Earth has great healing power for your body and mind.

Find a place to lie down on the ground somewhere, if you can, and experience yourself grounding into the Earth. You don't need to stay long on the ground, just long enough to feel yourself relaxing and coming present in your body.

Do avoid being in too much sun, however, as the extremely powerful solar flares that are currently erupting—although very important to the Earth's Ascension—are generally too strong for people to process easily at this time. And they may make your symptoms of disorientation worse.

Actually, the practice of grounding yourself is important to do fairly regularly when you're experiencing the waves of Ascension, whether you feel a sense of disorientation or not. It's not necessary to connect so entirely with the Earth each time. Just going barefoot on the Earth can give you a sense of connection and release.

And, in fact, you don't even have to go outside to ground yourself. You can simply call inwardly for the Earth's energy to envelop you and it will. It will come as a soft and gentle energy surrounding and filling you.

Another way to ground yourself is to visualize a "grounding cord" extending from your tailbone or your perineum down into the center of the Earth. Feel the little tug as it grounds you. And then send all thoughts and emotions that do not serve you down this cord into the Earth.

However you ground yourself, the Earth's energy can assist you during these times, as you experience the reawakening of your brain. Breathe this energy in and feel your profound connection to the Earth. It will heal you.

Chapter 7
Detachment

As you shift out of third-dimensional consciousness, another experience you may encounter is a sense of detachment toward almost everything in your life. In one way this can feel good—it's an experience of more distance from old patterns or issues that used to trigger you. And a sense of calm, as you view your life from a higher perspective.

Lack of Interest in Your Life

But, in another way, the detachment may be disconcerting or disorienting. For instance, you may be experiencing a growing lack of interest in your life, a sense of withdrawal from it. You might feel a lack of motivation to do anything new. You feel complete, finished, done with everything. There's nothing else out there that interests you to pursue anymore.

What can sometimes be upsetting is the loss of passion about things you used to care deeply about. How to keep going when there is no sense of passion about anything in your life? Passion is something that keeps us moving forward in life, helps us get up in the morning. Without passion, life can feel flat and lifeless.

And with this loss of passion and interest in life, a sense of boredom and impatience—and even depression—may arise. As always, don't be alarmed if this is happening. This too may show up as a part of the Ascension process.

Very naturally, you are letting go of the Third Dimension and all the interests and passions you've had on this level. You are being prepared to enter higher dimensions in which new interests and passions will arise. Or perhaps old ones will re-emerge in you, but it will be with new vision and clarity—and without your old ego agendas attached to them.

Be patient and know your sense of detachment is a sign that you're right on track. Relax and enjoy the sense of new freedom and openness that is also happening with the letting go of your old life. Allow the old dead interests and passions to simply fall away and see what arises in their place—which, among other things, may include an exquisite spaciousness.

Withdrawal from Relationships

Another form of detachment you may be experiencing is a feeling of withdrawal from your relationships with certain family members or friends—a sense that your connection to them is weakening or disappearing.

Perhaps you're finding you're not as interested anymore in things you used to share with them or in the stories of their drama or suffering. You're not getting involved in trying to "help" them like you were in the past. You're not as interested in spending so much time with them—you may even be finding them boring. You might be concerned about all this, wondering if you're becoming a less caring person.

Release of Karmic Bonds

This probably isn't so. The reasons for what you're experiencing are three-fold. One is that at this time, old karmic bonds are being released. Certain attachments that used to keep you and these people connected are now disappearing. There is less of a feeling of being bound to them. You've completed your contracts with them.

Vibrational Differences

Secondly, you're feeling the differences in your vibrations at this point. Because your consciousness has shifted to a new level of positive thought and awareness, people still living in a vibration of negativity, suffering and unconsciousness may no longer interest you. You might actually feel uncomfortable in your body when you're around them.

As described in Chapter 2, humanity is currently dividing into two general groups in the Fourth Dimension, according to frequency, each experiencing a different reality.

The first group includes those who are holding onto the darker and heavier thoughts, emotions and energies and are very threatened by change. Many of these, as times get rougher, may attempt to escape more into drugs, alcohol, sex and virtual reality. And many will eventually be leaving the earth plane as the earth's frequency continues to rise, to continue their third-dimensional experience elsewhere.

The second group consists of those who are choosing to make the transition to the Fifth Dimension. As part of this group, you will find that the reality you're living in is going to be quite different from that of certain other people you know. This will become more obvious as time goes on.

What you may have to come to terms with is that you might be leaving certain loved ones "behind". They may not be choosing to ascend at this time. But keep in mind that all Souls on Earth have been given the choice to ascend; some have chosen this path and some have not. If they haven't, you need to respect their choice.

It's important to allow each person their own path and to keep choosing your own. Stay detached—do not feel you need to "help" them get to the Fifth Dimension, as this attitude may pull you back from your own path.

Letting Go of *All* Attachments

The third reason you may be wanting to withdraw from familiar loved ones is that in order to enter the Fifth Dimension, you need to let go of all attachment, period—to all people or things outside of you. And the sense of detachment you're experiencing is just an indication that this is happening.

Do allow yourself to feel any sadness that may come up with this; honor your feelings. But don't wallow in them. Do what you can to commit yourself to your own choice of Ascension, and trust that those you leave behind are meant to walk a different path. They have chosen it in their own evolutionary journey. No one's choice is "better" or "worse" than another's; we each have our unique ways of finding our way back into full consciousness.

Greater Love

An interesting phenomenon that can happen as you experience yourself withdrawing from certain important relationships you've had is that, at the same time, you can actually be experiencing a greater love for these same people. But it's a new kind of love—one without attachment or demands. It's a love that is pure and unconditional in its support for them.

There are no expectations that your love be reciprocated—or that anything at all be returned. The love simply *is*. You can feel the person in your heart and you know that nothing they could ever say or do would change your love for them. You love them as a Soul—one you've probably known and loved for eons of time.

Experiencing the Void

At certain points during your journey through the higher Fourth Dimension, you may find yourself going through a period of living in what could be called the

"Void." This is not the Void that is sometimes described in spiritual teachings as the spacious and blissful reality that appears to one who has awakened beyond ego identification. The term here refers to a flat and rather barren state in which the ego self is experienced to be dying.

It's an empty kind of space that exists between what has been in your life and what will be. It's a natural and necessary passage in which you have the opportunity to release the past and open to a new you that is being birthed.

In the Void, detachment and withdrawal from the world become paramount. After perhaps attempting to recreate what you've experienced in your past and finding that it doesn't work anymore—there's simply no juice left in it—you eventually just begin withdrawing from your old life.

Your interest in the outer world eventually becomes almost nil. Your friendships seem to dwindle down to just the most core of relationships, and there's a desire to simply spend a lot of time home alone.

If this happens to you, remember it's just another aspect of the letting go of your old life and connections to your third-dimensional identity. It's actually a sign of progress along your path.

Usually we are brought into the Void when our ego has established too much control in our life. Our Soul leads us into the chaos and emptiness of the Void, so that we can let go of the ego-directed aspects of our life and find a new and deeper Self to live our lives from.

Time to Heal and Integrate

The Void also provides a time for deep healing to occur and for the integration of new, healthier patterns to be put into place. Without the usual outer distractions, all this can happen more rapidly and effectively. Often the ego initially resists the experience in the Void, but it even-

VIDYA FRAZIER

tually gives up, realizing that surrendering to the Soul's higher wisdom is its only choice.

Experiences in the Void differ for each person, but they generally involve a type of letting go—a releasing of chunks of ego-identification: parts of ourselves that no longer match the reality we're now living from, activities that no longer serve us, relationships that no longer fit who we've become.

There's also a falling-away of old ideas, beliefs and habits and constructs we've found to be untrue or meaningless. A sensation we might have is like that of a snake that's slid out of its old skin. We may try to crawl back in, but we really can't. Yet we have no clue where we do fit or what feels comfortable anymore. In general, we may experience an emptiness of self-ness, a blankness as to who we now are.

Simple Joys

And yet we may realize that there's a sweet simplicity that's appeared in our life. We find we are living more and more in the present moment and have slowed down enough to be able to fully experience small pleasures and joys we've missed before.

Much of what used to occupy our mind and time no longer interests us, so we discover the delight of these simple experiences that have always been there but we rarely took time to notice them before—such as the delicious warmth of sunlight shining through the window. Or the deep satisfaction of taking our first drink of cold water when we're thirsty.

A flower in our garden that has suddenly appeared overnight takes our breath away. We find ourselves stunned by the radiant beauty of the sunset, seeing colors we swear have never been part of a sunset before. A child's squeal of delight out our window arouses such a deep joy in us, we start laughing.

68

All of these things have always been part of our life; we've just not been present enough in the moment to experience them in their fullness.

Releasing of Old Patterns

And then at times, the landscape of the Void might also involve the experiencing of old emotions and patterns that seem to push their way to the surface out of nowhere. We may have no idea of why they've appeared or what we're supposed to do with them.

Depression

A common emotion that may arise for you at any point in the Ascension process—but perhaps more so while experiencing the Void—is depression. Often it has to do with loss. You are literally losing your past: certain relationships, important roles you've played for a long time, beliefs that you've held forever and thought were truth. You may even be losing your work or your home.

Your sense of purposeless and your questioning of everything you've believed in or wanted can sometimes make it difficult to keep going. And if people around you can't relate to all you're going through, you may well be also feeling loneliness.

Other times, there may be a pervasive dark mood that envelops you—and it may even seem to have nothing at all to do with you. It's just suddenly there—and then some time later, it's gone just as abruptly for no apparent reason.

This may be because you're tuning in to something happening in the collective consciousness somewhere in the world. As you begin to experience a greater sense of connection and unity with all of humanity, you will sometimes find yourself picking up on strong emotions felt by groups of people you don't even consciously know, such as people living in a country immersed in conflict or oppression. You somehow know something is going on with them and you're in some way connected to them.

If you sense this happening, feel the feelings and then consciously release them. Call light into your being and then ask it to be sent to those others you are connected to, whoever they might be. In doing this, you may feel the heaviness of the experience transform into a deep sense of love and compassion.

All this might sound depressing or frightening. But it need not be. Although your life can feel small and meaningless, you can simply keep in mind that this passage is all part of the journey and that all that has kept your third-dimensional identity together needs to be transformed. You can relax and just let everything take its course.

So long as you can avoid judging yourself for your empty, directionless life and not doing anything that feels important or valuable, you'll find that you can generally feel peaceful and accepting of what is happening.

Look for What's Emerging

In fact, if you watch carefully, you'll find that every time you experience a loss during a period in the Void, something new will be emerging. There may be a brief period of emptiness where the old relationship, belief, or sense of self is gone and there's nothing yet that's moved in to take its place. But if you're patient, you'll begin seeing that something new is indeed coming present in your life.

It might be something to replace what you've lost—or it could be a new-found sense of freedom, or maybe an opportunity to walk in a completely new and exciting direction in life. It will be something that couldn't have happened before you let go of something else.

Watch to see this dynamic: that as loss occurs, a new opening also occurs. As the old third-dimensional energies leave, new fifth dimensional energies are finding their way in.

Voids Always Eventually End

And remember too that your sojourn through the Void will not last forever. Although you may find yourself going through a number of Voids of varying lengths and intensity during your journey through the Fourth Dimension, at some point you'll find the feeling of the Void completely disappearing around you. A new life will open up for you and you'll discover a new you emerging, ready to create a new life.

You may find that there's "less" of the *you* you've always known as yourself walking around. Somewhere along the way, emotional and mental baggage has fallen away. There is less mind chatter happening. There's a sense of being newly born, fresh, with little outer covering or protection—and little need of it. You may experience a refreshing sense of childlike curiosity about the world, and a profound wonder at its beauty.

Keep all this in mind and your journey through the Void can be a deeply fulfilling time. In fact, if you remember you're in the middle of an extraordinary birth process, it can be one of joy, self-discovery and anticipation.

Keys for Navigating the Ascension Process

Chapter 8
Riding the Waves of Ascension

As may be clear, the experience of Ascension is not a static one. In many ways, it's a dance, a dance of letting go of old, limiting energies of the Third Dimension—and at the same time, opening to the new and expansive energies of the higher Fourth and Fifth Dimensions.

And because the Ascension energies seem to come in waves, it's also a dance that has numerous pauses in it when everything seems to calm down and smooth out for a while.

During these times, you have the opportunity to relax and become aware of all the exciting changes that may have happened within you. Perhaps you'll find that you seem to be able to access many things in the new "operating system" of the Fourth Dimension more easily, such as love, inner peace, or laughter. Perhaps you'll realize that if your mood does grow gloomy, it's harder to stay in that state of mind than it was in the past.

Negative emotions aren't as dense or powerful as they used to be. You may find that it's hard to hold onto anger or sadness for any length of time, and it's much easier to shift your attention to something positive or pleasurable. Indeed, sometimes, even in the middle of a painful situation, you may suddenly experience a powerful moment of pure joy, or feel your heart well up with gratitude for something.

You may also find that it's easier to recognize that your depressed mood has to do with the story you're telling yourself about what's happening in your life, and that you can just as easily tell yourself another more positive story. Or maybe no story at all! It's all a lot simpler to do these things with the new fourth-dimensional energies streaming onto the planet.

At the same time, when a wave of Ascension energy does hit you and you feel yourself grasping for familiar ground to stand on, it's helpful to have keys that can assist you to stay in balance, tools that can be touchstones for bringing you back to a sense of stability.

Look Within for Security

There are times you might experience anxiety due to a sense that there's no longer any security present in your life that used to come from a marriage, a secure bank account, a family, a group of friends who loved you—or whatever. And now with the loss of one or more of these outer supports you've always had, you feel adrift in a sea of change with nothing secure to hold onto.

Perhaps you also feel at times a sense of being constantly pushed ahead too quickly, that you're being compelled to let go of old relationships, emotions, and beliefs, one after another without a break. You're constantly being moved out of your comfort zone—you barely catch your breath and you're being pushed to the next level of letting go.

When this happens, you have the opportunity to discover something very important: that the only true security comes from within you. It does not originate from anything outside of you. And often, for you to finally discover this, all the outer supports you mistakenly thought were keeping you safe will disappear, at least for a while.

So the answer is to look within for your security. This may be difficult, though, when it feels like only chaos exists within you—when familiar parts of yourself are falling away and new unfamiliar parts are appearing.

But if you can look past these changing aspects of yourself, you will realize that these are just parts of your personality self that are shifting. If you can look more deeply, you will discover that there's an essential YOU inside that is not changing.

It's the YOU that was the same when you were three years old, fifteen and thirty years old. It is, and always has been, the YOU that is real. It is also the one that has always been leading you through life, whether you've been aware of it or not.

Trust the Higher YOU

You are being called to trust this Higher YOU. See if you can trust that it knows exactly what it's doing in bringing about the changes in your life, including the losses that initially seem painful. Know that the things you are losing are essential for you to lose so as to prepare you for entering the Fifth Dimension.

It is bringing up old issues and emotions for you to finally face and let go of. And it is bringing in new awarenesses and understandings that may initially feel threatening to you; but they are part of the new fifth-dimensional consciousness coming in.

Letting Go

If it starts feeling chaotic and unstable for you in your life, you can learn to ride the wave. See if you can be willing to let go of all old beliefs and judgments about yourself, as well as any attitudes or distorted perspectives on life that are not based in truth. Do your best to let go of old relationships that are no longer working.

If you are losing a long-time mode of making a living or a comfortable home you've enjoyed for years, see if you can make the leap of faith to simply let them go. Trust that if this is happening, it's probably what is necessary for your awakening. And know that you will be taken care of in the process in ways you might never have thought of before.

Realize that the more you try to hang onto things that are disappearing, the more the universe will push back on you. Trust the process. Finding out what is really essential to your Being, you can discover who you are beyond all your ego identities, attachments, and limited beliefs about yourself.

This process of letting go may bring basic survival fears up in you. It can feel like a stripping away of who you are. But remember, it's only a stripping away of who you *think* you are. It's a dismantling of the ego structure you've taken to be your "self".

The good news is that you'll find that throughout this whole deconstruction period, the essential YOU will remain intact. In fact, this true reality of who you are will finally be able to shine forth in all its glory. You will experience a thrilling sensation of freedom, when all of who you are *not* has been released.

Ascension into the Fifth Dimension is truly a form of rebirth. And in order to be reborn, you need to die first to what you have been in the past. In a way, it's not all that different from the physical dying process in the third-dimensional experience: in the end, you have to let go of everything. You have no choice.

If you can move into trust of your Ascension process, you'll find that the wave you're riding into the Fifth Dimension is bringing you to a place of greater security, peace, and joy than you can even imagine.

Purification

The intense emotional states you may at times experience can be seen as a process of *purification*. To enter the Fifth Dimension, all that is not clear and positive within you must eventually come up to be released so that you are able to live in the higher vibration of that dimension.

In order to match this vibration, you must be vibrating with the energies of love, peace, freedom, and confidence. You must know, beyond a doubt, that you are a powerful multi-dimensional being. After thousands of years of living with such emotions as fear, hatred, and anger—all part of third-dimensional consciousness—you are being called to release these emotions.

Flow with the Transformational Process

The key is to not fight any of this. Instead, attempt to relax into it. Purification is going to happen, whether or not you feel you're ready for it. Resistance will just make it more painful. See if you can trust that what's happening is absolutely necessary and is occurring in the best way possible. Move consciously into its flow, let go, and allow yourself to burn.

Something you can do to help balance yourself when in the midst of emotional upheaval during this purification process is to purposely slow your pace with everything you're doing. Stop if you can and take some deep breaths when it gets overwhelming.

Come often into the present moment—it's the only place to find balance. Give up multi-tasking for a while; focus on one conscious thought at a time. And engage in an activity that brings you peace, regardless of what else you think may be pressing on you.

Also keep in mind that you're in the middle of experiencing a very rapid transformational process. This stuff coming up isn't the normal, run-of-the-mill stuff you're used to dealing with. This is a butterfly process. And a cocoon is always a mushy mess on the inside. Be patient with yourself.

Concentrate on relaxing into the pain when it arises. Don't argue with it, resist it, or try to change it. Don't try to push it out either. Just gently let it be. Focus on trust. Be willing to let old patterns and emotions that seem to be leaving fall away. With deep intention to see it through, the intensity of your reactive emotions can eventually calm down.

And at some point, it can be helpful to ask yourself what it is that you're being invited to see or learn from the situation. Is there something you're being encouraged to release? Is there something you're resisting that you need to embrace? Look for the gift being offered to you, as there always is one hidden within all challenging situations.

Embracing All That Is

In fact, an important key to making it easier to meet whatever may be arising for you during your Ascension process is understanding that all of life is to be embraced—*all* of it. All emotions, negative as well as positive. Resisting what is uncomfortable will not work.

Experiencing all of what is happening to you is what you are here to do in life—to experience all of it, whether it's pleasant or painful—and anything in between.

Embracing all experiences in your life might be more difficult to do lately if you're having more unpleasant experiences than you're used to. You may be finding that certain situations are getting out of control in surprising ways. All this is to be expected in the process of Ascension.

The important thing, however, is to pay attention when these things happen. You will probably find yourself automatically resisting what is occurring—both the situation and the emotions arising within yourself. This too is to be expected. It's what third-dimensional consciousness dictates:

"At all costs, resist anything that feels threatening, painful or unpleasant."

This is an approach that the human race has taken for thousands of years. Despite the fact that resistance doesn't even work to relieve pain, it is a survival mechanism that the human ego has nonetheless used for a long, long time.

At this point, however, this survival mechanism is no longer appropriate. In order to flow smoothly into the energies of the higher dimensions, it's necessary to learn how to not only stop resisting what is painful in your life—but to actually learn how to embrace it, with open arms.

Embracing Life is Not a Passive Approach

This is not a passive approach to life. It's not about resigning yourself to whatever is happening to you, acting as a victim or a doormat. And it's not about staying stuck in painful situations.

Embracing all of life actually involves a very active, conscious approach to life in which you stay awake, continuously paying close attention to your thoughts, emotions and reactions. Not in a stressful way—just an alert and conscious one.

It's also an attitude full of trust—trust that all that is happening to you and arising within you, is absolutely perfect. It's what you in your higher consciousness are purposely bringing forth for you to experience at this time.

If it's a pleasant or joyful experience, then this is what is exactly right for you in the moment. If it's a painful or unpleasant experience, then that is what is appropriate. It's happening so you may experience it fully—and then release it.

Don't even resist resistance when it comes up. It's an old friend. Just gently focus on moving away from it into an attitude of acceptance. You don't have to like or enjoy what's happening; you just need to be open to accept and welcome it.

Love Will Diffuse Your Pain

And, when you are able, open your arms fully to whatever is happening and embrace it. You will discover that your love of anything difficult brought into your life will eventually diffuse all pain around it. You will see, indeed, that enough love will truly turn all suffering around. At some point, with enough love, you will even feel grateful for all your painful experiences, for they will have assisted you into greater freedom.

Each experience, if fully embraced, is one more step on your journey into the higher dimensions. Keep in mind that you are in the process of both dying and being reborn. It's only natural that you're going to feel a lot of intense emotion at times.

With time, and with trust, it will become easier to navigate these new waters. And you may even begin, with great abandon, to enjoy them.

Healing Silence

One of the best things you can give yourself when you're experiencing intense emotions is silence. It's also crucial to find silence when you're experiencing a lot of noise and drama in the lives of others around you. See if you can find a place of silence for yourself, a sanctuary where there's as little distraction as possible, and spend time there alone when you can.

When you move into silence, you may become aware of a lot of energetic activity taking place inside. Pay attention to that and move with it. If you feel tears coming up, let them have expression. Something old and no longer useful may be arising to be released. Or something deep within you may be emerging and wanting to express itself.

These times of clearing will come and go during the coming few years. When you feel this process happening, listen to the silence. It will assist you in your process.

There is a wisdom the silence can impart to you that far surpasses any wisdom you may gain through the medium of words.

Ask for Help

It's important to remember when you're going through hard times that you don't have to tough it out on your own. You can ask for help. Be aware that even if you're someone who's never had to ask for help before, these are times that are different from ever before and can be very challenging.

It can be difficult to process painful emotions on your own. You probably could do it, but it's not necessary. Don't let pride stand in your way. Ask for help from those around you—friends or family members who may be understanding—or someone in a more professional relationship.

You can also ask help from the invisible realms: from your spirit guides, celestial beings, archangels. They are present, waiting to be asked.

Assistance from Star Beings

You can even ask for help from extraterrestrial Star Beings. These beings from many places in the universe are currently gathering around our planet, ready to play their roles in the Ascension process that both humanity and the Earth are undergoing. They are here to help us in every way they can to move from third-dimensional consciousness into fifth.

They are eager to help; but to obtain their assistance, you must ask for it. Nothing is too large or too small to ask them. You can ask for spiritual guidance. You can ask for more energy. You can ask for help in finding a love partner, a new home, new work, more money, better health. If it's for your highest good, they will assist in bringing you whatever you need, so you can put as much focus as possible on raising your vibration to a higher level.

Do not think you are being petty, selfish or materialistic in asking for assistance in making your life and environment more pleasant and comfortable. If a sense of greater comfort affords you more relaxation so that you can focus on your spiritual Ascension more fully, then it may be appropriate that you have those things that will help you do that.

When you first call these beings in, sit in silence. Let them make themselves known to you in whatever way they will. You may hear them, see them, or simply sense their presence. Trust what you are perceiving; know that they are there with you, whether your mind is sure or not.

Open to their love for you. If you're really allowing it, you may initially experience their love as almost overwhelming. Don't worry; they won't push. They understand the third-dimensional limitations you've been living under and your unfamiliarity with experiencing unconditional love in this dimension.

It's just that they can see you in a clear way that few human beings (yourself included) ever can—and what they see is a magnificent being. So their love for you is both immediate and natural.

If you are open to really letting them in, you'll find they have the ability to see *all* of who you are, including all you might label as "flaws". They won't perceive them that way, however. They know that everything, including what you may see as imperfect, is actually absolutely perfect, as it is. There is no judgment—just a clear seeing and a loving acceptance of who you are. You can simply relax with them.

When you ask for their help, be specific. For instance, if you're having difficulty in a relationship, don't simply say "I need help in this relationship." Say "Help me open my heart to this person and experience forgiveness." Or "Help me stand up for myself and speak my truth."

Be aware that these Star Beings are also learning from you. This is a mutual exchange. They are offering their services to you as part of their own plan of Soul evolution.

You may find that the Star Beings that come to you are part of a galactic inter-dimensional team you're a part of, designed to achieve a mission on the planet at this time. You may begin realizing you have a Soul contract with them that you made before incarnating this time around.

Take time to simply commune with your galactic team members without words. They are beings, just like you—they've simply taken a journey in different parts of the universe than you have. But they truly are your brothers and sisters.

Feel your heart expand with love for them, as you allow them more and more into your life—and watch the magic begin to unfold.

Chapter 9
Opening to Love

In many ways, Ascension is teaching us about love. Not the kind of limited and often distorted love that has been prevalent in the Third Dimension—an emotion that is often confused with need, desire, or lust. But love simply as a natural quality of being that exists in the higher dimensions.

This kind of spiritual love is what we experience at times when we feel ourselves able to fully self-source, when we've stopped needing to feel loved and cared about by others in order to feel okay about ourselves. We experience this love, simply because it is our inherent nature. We discover that love is not something we have: it's what we actually *are*.

Identity Shift from Head to Heart

In order to fully know your inherent nature as love in an ongoing way, you will likely feel at some point in your Ascension process that your sense of identity begins shifting from your head to your Heart. "Heart" in this context, of course, does not simply mean the physical organ in your chest—although it includes it. Nor does it only refer to a space you may feel in your chest when you experience emotions—although it includes this too.

Your Heart is actually a huge, dynamic energetic field that is centered in your entire chest and sometimes extends many feet all around you. It is a part of you that is an essential aspect of your Being that has not had full expression in most of your third-dimensional experiences. It has sometimes been referred to as the "sacred" Heart.

When activated, the energy of your Heart can be strongly felt by others; it can affect not only individuals, but whole groups of people. It can help to raise the vibration in situations you're in. It can assist the healing in both yourself and others.

At some point, as you move into ever higher levels of the Fourth Dimension, you may find yourself actually beginning to "think" with your Heart, rather than with your rational mind. You'll actually feel thoughts coming out of your chest area. And you'll experience your mind moving into the role of simply helping you with the mundane tasks of functioning in the physical world—its original purpose.

The power of the Heart is barely recognized today, although the HeartMath Institute is currently conducting breakthrough research on the physiological, mental and emotional effects of the Heart and finding the benefits of establishing coherence between the mind and Heart. As time goes on, it seems the power of the Heart will become more and more recognized, as the new age humanity is walking into is in many ways the age of the Heart.

Heart Opening Experiences

If you have had powerful Heart-opening experiences, you know there is truly no feeling like the experience of a fully-opened Heart. You're familiar with the enormous waves of love that can flood your Being, rocking your entire sense of who you are. You know the indescribable bliss that can envelop you as a deep sense of peace pervades your Being, along with a feeling of being one with all that exists.

These kinds of experiences are gifts that are sometimes given to us, seemingly out of nowhere. But if you are generally used to living life with your Heart not fully open (like most people), know that the higher frequencies of Light coming onto the Earth today are working to help open your Heart fully on a permanent basis. In a way, you really have no choice. If you're going to move with the Earth into the Fifth Dimension, your Heart is going to open.

This is because the portal to your Soul exists in your Heart, the doorway you're passing through to become your fifth-dimensional Self. Your Soul is clearing this pathway for you. And it knows perfectly how to do this.

Living from your Heart

So how can you consciously live in a more Heart-centered place on an ongoing basis? It's often difficult to simply shift your sense of identification from the rational mind to the Heart, just because you want to. Spending thousands of years with the mind as your source of identity can be a hard habit to break.

But you can start by simply noticing when you're feeling identified solely with your rational mind and perceiving yourself and life through this limited and distorted lens. Remind yourself that this is not who you are. You are not your thoughts, your beliefs, your judgments or your emotions. You are not anything so small and contained.

Consciously be aware of how it feels when you're identified with your mind, how unempowered you can feel—and how dull, painful, and even pointless life can seem. This is because the rational mind's perspective is extremely limited, designed only for third-dimensional living. It doesn't understand the experience or the wisdom of the Heart.

Once you realize all this, ask inwardly for help. Bring your awareness to your physical heart. Feel it beating in your chest. Take a deep breath and relax into yourself. Sense the energy that encompasses your Heart—the larger vibrating field around it.

Focus gently on this area of your Being. What do you experience there?

Painful Emotions May Arise

Sometimes when you stop to simply focus on a closed feeling in your Heart, you may experience the force of unfelt emotions stuck in your chest. These are feelings that need to be felt before experiencing the full power of your love. It's been said that the Heart is never really "closed", although it can feel that way. It's just that unfelt emotions can block our experience of it.

If you feel emotions arising in you, move into gentle compassion for yourself. Ask your Heart what it is you need to do to release the emotions. If your Heart initially feels really closed, you may find yourself in tears for a while as you release the energy of these painful emotions.

You might feel fear about this process when it begins, wondering if the painful emotions arising will overwhelm you. It can sometimes actually feel like your physical heart is breaking open. Or you may remember other times when your Heart was opened and you felt an unbearable vulnerability.

Know that, in the Ascension process, the painful emotions that arise will not overwhelm you. They're just coming up *to be released*—to make room for more love to awaken in your Being. If you feel caught in the feelings, repeat to yourself over and over: *They're leaving, they're leaving*. Consciously allow the energy of the emotions to flow through and out of you.

Remember that once they're released, the love you're seeking has the opportunity to emerge. It may take a while for painful emotions to release; it's a process that can be a mixed experience of joy, pain, fear and relief. But it can eventually resolve into a kind of bliss deeply infused with love.

Vulnerability is Not Weakness

Remember that a feeling of vulnerability is the natural result of Heart opening. But this does not have to be frightening or make you feel weak. On the contrary, your very vulnerability is your strength.

As you allow yourself to relax into the vulnerability, you will discover that who you truly are cannot be affected by anything—and certainly not by other people's actions, emotions, or words. Ironically, utter vulnerability is the most powerful protection you have.

When you fully allow your vulnerability, you will find that the pathway into the deeper recesses of your Heart opens. As this occurs, a clearer, more positive experience of who you are emerges. You become aware of the love that is always present, just waiting for you to experience it.

The Importance of Loving Yourself

Perhaps the most important focus of opening to love during these times is learning to truly love yourself— totally, unconditionally—just as you are. In fact, loving yourself may be the most essential thing you need to learn if you are going to enter the Fifth Dimension. You must first believe yourself worthy of love and respect—and act in all ways knowing this worth. You need to fully embrace and care for ALL that you are.

You've probably heard it said before in certain spiritual teachings that you are perfect exactly as you are. And that you are lovable exactly as you are. But perhaps you haven't been able to really believe this, that there are too many things you see in yourself that could be improved or that need to be different before you can be perfect or loved totally for who you are.

The Mind's Misperception of Perfection

Understand that your inherent perfection has nothing to do with this limited perception of perfection. It's the nature of the mind to hold a concept of "perfection" and a whole array of opinions and judgments of qualities it believes to be good and bad or right and wrong.

This is just how the human mind has developed in the third-dimensional world. In its natural limitation, the mind cannot perceive the perfection of who you are—the magnificence of what you are as a Soul, a spiritual being. It cannot see beyond the level on which it exists.

Nor can it truly understand that you, as an evolving being, are always going to be in a constant process of changing, learning, growing, and awakening. You will never achieve the mind's limited, distorted concept of perfection. Nor, when you finally begin realizing your true perfection, will you ever want to. It's too limited and too based in illusion.

But even your mind, with all its illusions and limitations, is something to love. It's an amazing tool. Realize that it's always done its very best trying to keep you safe. It doesn't know that you no longer need it for that purpose—and it needs time to adapt to all that is happening to you in your Ascension process. So be gentle with your mind; understand its limitations and the ways in which it may not be as competent as you might have thought it was.

Embrace All of Who You Are

Instead explore living from your Heart and turning a gentle compassionate love toward yourself. If you have trouble knowing what this kind of love might feel like, think about how you may feel toward small children and animals. This is the kind of natural unconditional love you need to give yourself.

Let this love seep into every cell in your body. Let it flow into your emotions and your mind. Accept and embrace ALL of who you are. You don't have to *like* everything about yourself. You just need to accept that your qualities are part of who you are for now. And because they're part of you, you can love them.

See that all aspects of your being—ALL of them—every "flaw", "shortcoming", and "mistake" you see—are expressions of the Divine. And the Divine does not judge Itself. It only knows to love Itself.

Putting Yourself First

If you've been on a spiritual path for a while—or have simply considered yourself to be a "good" and "unselfish" person—you might react to hearing that it's now time to do something that Quantum Healer Dell Morris has called *putting yourself first*. This may sound like a swing back into a selfish lower mode of consciousness that rings of "me first" or "looking out for Number One."

But that is not what putting yourself first is referring to in the context of finding your way into the Fifth Dimension. And it's something that is essential to learn.

Traditional spiritual teachings have focused on the importance of learning how to step out of selfishness and to practice loving other people. They've focused on the importance of forgiveness, compassion and being of service to others. This has all been very important for moving into spiritual maturity.

But it's now time to raise your vibration even higher than this to a level beyond focusing on being of service to others. This is not about relinquishing your compassion for others or serving them in ways that feel appropriate. It's simply important now that your focus, in every way possible, be on loving yourself. It's time to stop thinking this is a selfish attitude. Remember, if you are truly loving yourself, you are all the more able to love others.

Ask yourself: How have I not been taking care of myself? How have I been judging myself? How have I denied myself the love and compassion I give to others?

Refusing to Sell Out for Approval

For instance, how often do you deny your own truth just to keep the peace with others? How often do you go along with what others want, because it appears easier—only to feel that you've somehow betrayed yourself in the process?

How often have you not quite told the truth to someone, for fear you won't be loved, included, respected? Or for fear of making things awkward or hurting someone's feelings? How often have you stayed quiet in order to avoid someone's anger?

All of these kinds of decisions are ways of selling out for approval. They're ways of choosing fear over love. It's time to choose love—and most importantly, self-love. It's time to start putting your own needs first, always, in every situation—time to break out of any programmed conditioning that tells you that making yourself your priority is being "self-centered" or "selfish".

Sometimes this includes learning how to say No, when you really feel the NO inside of you. It means trusting this NO when it appears, trusting that it is right both for you and the person asking something of you. And it means setting and keeping boundaries with people who are making uncomfortable or inappropriate demands on you.

You can feel the rightness of these decisions to say No when your body breathes a sigh of relief and relaxes—despite what your anxious mind might be saying.

With every decision you make in regard to doing something with or for someone else, ask yourself, "Is this for my highest good? Am I valuing myself, taking care of myself?"

Become aware of automatic decisions to simply do something because someone is asking you to. Think about it first. If necessary, let them know you'll get back to them about it. Give yourself time to get clear on whether saying Yes is really what is best for you.

If you've been a "nice" person that others have always been able to count on, this can be a hard habit to break. It can bring up fears about people not liking you anymore. Be conscious about breaking this habit. Know that, in truth, if you begin to truly take care of yourself out of respect and love for yourself, other people are more likely to both respect and love you more. It's just what happens.

People may even actually begin to love you more for who you *are*, rather than for what you can do for them. And even more importantly, their love and approval of you won't be that important to you anymore, anyway—because your own love and valuing of yourself will be what matters.

Taking Complete Responsibility for Yourself

True self-love includes taking complete responsibility for yourself. It means taking care of your own emotional needs. It means respecting and valuing yourself, and not depending on anyone else to respect or value you so you can feel good about yourself.

As difficult as it may seem at times, you need to trust that if you take care of yourself first in a situation, all else will fall into place as it should. This takes faith, because it may not seem this is happening at first. Some people may be unhappy or angry with you, if they're used to your putting *them* first.

But if you are taking care of yourself, while staying open to your love for them, they will eventually see that they need to take responsibility for their own emotional needs. This is appropriate. And as you take care of yourself first, you will also be modeling to them what they may need to do for themselves.

This doesn't mean you stop taking care of others when they're in need. There are obvious times when your help is very appropriate and necessary. It simply means it's time to become aware of what you are responsible for—and what other people are responsible for. Fifth-dimensional consciousness includes taking total responsibility for ourselves, for our own emotions and actions—and not for those of others.

In essence, these times we're in really are not so much about "saving the world". As has been pointed out often, if we are not "saved" inside of us—if we are still battling ourselves, feeling anger, fear, hatred, and judgment inside—how can we save anyone else?

We need to first bring true peace, love and harmony into our own consciousness—and then see what "saving" may be appropriate to do in the world.

Chapter 10
Learning Trust

If you learn nothing else on your journey into the Fifth Dimension, it's going to be trust. In particular, trust of the Unknown...trust that you're being guided, no matter how alone you may feel...trust that whatever is happening to you, as unsettling and unfamiliar as it may be at times, is absolutely right for you.

Over time, you will see that you are traveling on the "road less traveled". There are not yet a lot of road signs where you are going, nor obvious pointers as to which way to go. Unidentified crossroads may confuse you; apparent dead ends may cause you to doubt. You may feel lost for a while until you get your bearings again.

Another analogy describing these times, especially when we find ourselves struggling to hold on to our old lives and identities, is one given to us by Indigenous Elders. The analogy is of a river we've all been swimming along in, in our lives. Till now we've generally been swimming close to shore where the current is relatively gentle, stopping off here and there along the way, taking a rest and setting up house for awhile in different places.

They tell us that it's now time to move away from the shores of the river—to not hang on to anything there anymore. It's time, rather, to swim out to the middle of the river and just let the powerful currents there take us. It's time to surrender to the river and trust it will take us where we need to go.

You are Being Guided

These analogies may bring up fear and uncertainty. But fear not. As you become more and more aware on your Ascension journey, you will see that you are being guided, held and protected—and that you are always being kept on course in the right direction, in right timing.

When in doubt, avoid listening to other people's opinions; they may not be familiar with your unique path and may point you back onto old familiar roads that are no longer right for you. Instead, trust your intuition. Stop and listen inwardly when confused. It's okay to stop for awhile until you get clear.

Remember that before you incarnated this time around, you knew full well what would be happening on the Earth during your sojourn here. You fully understood and gratefully signed up for it and all it would entail. And you trusted that all would fall into place as you made your way along your journey.

Now you must trust that decision you made. You must trust that you are being guided every step of the way—not only by your Higher Self, but also by your guides, celestial beings, spiritual masters and galactic beings here specifically to assist in the Ascension process. They're all here with you, whether you're yet aware of them or not.

Developing Faith

One of the signposts that you may be resisting where your Ascension path is taking you is when the feeling of struggle arises. If you find yourself attempting to achieve something and it's clear over and over again that it's not working, stop. It's important for you to cease striving and give up trying to make something happen that isn't going to happen.

Instead, assume that something else is wanting to happen and surrender to this probability. Watch to see what else may unfold. You may initially feel that what's happening is not right, not what's "supposed" to be happening. But, if you have faith and stay tuned to your inner knowing, you'll realize in time that it's exactly perfect. You'll see that everything coming into your life is what will help you ascend in the fastest, smoothest way.

You will begin to see this more clearly if you shift your perception from your mind to your Heart. Intuitively, you will sense the rightness of all occurrences and experiences in your life as they happen.

Choice of Survival or Faith

During these times as you travel through the Fourth Dimension, you will often have the choice of two different approaches to life: the third-dimensional choice of survival, and the fifth-dimensional choice of faith.

The third-dimensional mode of "survival" in this context doesn't just apply to getting food and shelter and other material needs met. It refers to a generally unconscious approach to life in general in which you may be trying to be in control of everything in your life.

There's a belief that you'd better make sure everything in your life is in place or you won't survive: you'd better have enough money (which may mean a reliable job, money in the bank, or a close relationship with someone who will support you), and good relationships to feel emotional support when you need it.

You may not look at relying on these things as a mode of survival, but they are. You've just lived with them for so long that they don't seem to be a form of survival.

Looking Inward for What you Need

The important thing to realize is that when you're in the mode of survival, you are looking outside yourself for all you need. You're using your limited third-dimensional mind to determine how you're going to maintain yourself here on the planet: how to get the things you need to physically survive, and how to get the emotional support you believe you need from people around you. And this can keep you in a continuous state of anxiety, especially as you come to realize in the end that you may have very little control over outer conditions.

As you move toward fifth-dimensional consciousness, you will find that you need to let go of this limited perspective. You'll see that your belief that your needs are going to be met by things and situations you've set up outside you and by people you've brought into your life isn't working anymore.

If you are strongly attached to believing that these things are responsible for your sense of safety and survival, you will probably be given the opportunity to find out that they are not. Many of these outer supports may disappear (either temporarily or permanently) to show you this.

If, for example, you lose your job, your life savings, or an important relationship, know that it is this learning dynamic that may be what is operating. Instead of panicking, see if you can drop inside yourself and align with a faith that you will find the means of survival in other ways—perhaps in ways that will bring you an even greater sense of joy and freedom.

Reliance on Faith

In fifth-dimensional consciousness, there is no reliance on anything in the outer world for a sense of safety or survival. There is only reliance on faith—faith that life will bring you absolutely everything you need, when you need it.

Eventually faith is replaced by a secure knowing, a certainty based on your own experience that you are always taken care of. But until that fully develops, faith is what you need to rely on, a trust in a higher power—whether you name this God, Spirit, Source or your Higher Self. You trust that it is guiding your life and taking care of you with utmost compassion and wisdom.

This doesn't mean that you just sit on your couch and watch TV all day long, trusting that you're being taken care of (although it might mean this for a while, if this is appropriate or necessary for you). It just means that you have faith that you will be shown the way to live, support yourself, and find not only a sense of security —but also a sense of well-being.

It may actually mean that you gear up to explore doing all the more out in the world to take care of yourself. But your motivation will come from a calm intuitive nudging to do those things, not from an anxiety arising from your mind.

With faith as your guide, you will find synchronicities blooming all around you; little miracles will become commonplace in your life. And the more you live from this place of faith, the stronger your faith will become. You'll see that there is nothing outside in the world that is permanent or dependable for your safety or survival. But with the faith you have inside, it won't matter.

Learning to live fully from a place of faith is not always easy. But the relaxation and the freedom from fear you experience when you begin to achieve this are monumental and will change your entire experience of life.

Practice Now Before It Really Counts

There may come a time in the months and years ahead when the collective consciousness of the planet will be greatly challenged by events that may take place, events that might topple any sense of financial and physical security.

There are economists and visionaries alike who are predicting major collapses in the near future in the world's economy and in governmental structures. Since humanity is in the process of transitioning very rapidly into a fifth-dimensional consciousness, it makes sense that we may be seeing some chaos in old, dysfunctional institutions and governing structures before new ones are established. And, if so, we may also see some major panicking going on in response to all the changes and uncertainty that humanity will be experiencing.

Create Your "Eye of the Storm"

If all this happens, fear may reign for a while around you in your world. It will be important for you to create your own personal inner "eye of the storm", in order to not take on the vibration of fear that may be storming around you—a clear, still place within in which you can maintain an experience of trust and peace. You can see it as a fifth-dimensional bubble you can function in that is not affected by the third and lower fourth-dimensional fear vibrations around you.

It's always best to practice for this kind of situation ahead of time, to prepare and develop a quiet place of trust inside you *before* you need it. You can give yourself practice with smaller things at first.

For example, if you hear at some point that you're going to need some medical care in the near future and you have no idea where the money for it will come from, move into trust about it. Know that the medical care is important, and so of course it will be taken care of. Have faith, an actual expectation, that the money will be provided. You may be surprised at how this faith will actually bring to you the money you need.

Stay in the Present Moment

A major key in learning to stay balanced and out of fear about survival is to live in the present moment. You may know that your mortgage is due tomorrow, but you are not living in tomorrow yet—you're here, right now. If you sit and worry today about what might happen tomorrow, you will attract more worry tomorrow.

However, if you can hold a focus on the present moment, you can create a different scenario for yourself. You can affirm, "Right now, I'm fine. I have a roof over my head, food to eat. Let me ground myself, clear my mind and enter into trust. Let me take some deep breaths and see what my options are." In doing this, possibilities can then begin to flow into the clear and open space you've created.

Magic Happens

In actuality, when you truly practice trust, it can seem like magic is happening in your life. If you choose to live with higher vibrations of Light anchored within you, you will begin to see that things always work out in your life—you're somehow always taken care of. If you believe you'll be taken care of, you will be. This is how the universe works.

At times the most unforeseen, miraculous-seeming things can happen when you're facing what seems to be a disastrous situation. In one moment, you're feeling desperate and hopeless—and in the next, something totally unexpected happens that completely turns the disaster around.

If you think about it, you may have already had this kind of situation happen in your life. Remember it. Know it can happen again. And again. You really never know what is around the corner that may "save" you.

There are so many possibilities beyond what you can now imagine of how something can happen. It really makes sense to let the universe/God/Soul take care of it for you, rather than forcing your rational mind to make its scrambling, ineffective attempts at solving the problem, when the solution is so obviously beyond its capabilities.

Trusting Your Inner Guidance

One thing that can be difficult in the process of learning to trust is dealing with the self-doubt that can arise when important decisions need to be made. Most of us growing up in the Third Dimension were not encouraged to make decisions from our own natural place of knowing. It was assumed that we needed to learn from others what was right and wrong and which decisions were best to take. Our inherent inner guidance system was not acknowledged or valued.

We were also taught that the best way to make decisions was by using our rational mind, which has a natural tendency toward fear and distrust of the world around us. As a result, we were taught to doubt ourselves and our own judgment, and as adults we can still struggle with doubt when making important decisions.

If you're having a hard time making a major life decision, you may find yourself simply jumping back and forth between the pros and cons of each option and getting nowhere. The key when this happens is to understand that you're using the wrong tool for this. You're using your rational mind.

The mind can be a good tool if you're making small, mundane decisions, such as what to buy for dinner, when to set a doctor's appointment, or what to wear to a dinner party. For more important decisions in life, however, the mind is woefully inadequate.

In discovering this, you may find yourself turning to other people for their opinions on your situation. Inevitably, they will give them to you. Sometimes it can be helpful to hear what others have to say; but often these opinions can just add to your confusion.

You might hear at some point the advice: "Just follow your heart." This can sound good. But what does that really mean?

When you go into your heart, you may simply be accessing your emotional heart, as opposed to your sacred Heart—and you might initially encounter emotions and desires about your situation, such as fear, anger, and greed. This can be helpful in telling you something about your emotional state. But your emotional heart is probably not the best guide for helping you make an important life decision.

You may also hear the advice: "Follow your intuition." Again this can sound good. But perhaps you aren't sure that what you hear inside is actually your intuition. Maybe it's just your mind, your inner child, your inner judge—or whatever else is in there. How can you tell?

Tuning into Your Sacred Heart

Especially now, during this time of Ascension, when you're making an important decision in life, where you need to focus is on your Sacred Heart. It is here that your answers reside.

Take time to sit quietly and go within to find the wisdom of your Heart. Ask for guidance; set an intention to receive the answer. Then place a hand on your chest and focus on this area. Breathe deeply and move within until you're in a quiet space.

If you initially encounter emotions here, feel them—gently and directly. Then see if you can move to an even deeper place, beyond thought and feeling into the stillness that's always present inside.

Asking for Right Action

When you're settled in the silence, focus on your question and ask: "What is right action in this situation?" Note that this is the important term: *right action*. You're not asking what you want or what will make you happy. And you're not asking what you *should* do.

It's a question about what is right, what is appropriate for you at this time, what decision or action is spiritually accurate for you at this point on your path of Ascension.

Ask the question as neutrally as possible. Ask for clarity and openness to whatever the answer may be, without any attachment to outcome. Then sit and wait quietly and patiently. You may hear an answer, see an image of some kind, or experience a feeling in your body. Or a clear knowing may just suddenly occur.

Sometimes if you ask a yes or no question, the answer will come simply as a physical sensation. A *No* may manifest as a tightness in your gut, and a *Yes* may be a sense of immediate relaxation in the same area. At times, if you're feeling in tune with your inner guidance, a sudden urge to get up and take an action will occur. This is usually a bodily response to an inner message to act.

The Answer May be Delayed

Sometimes the answer won't come at the time you're asking the question. Be patient if you feel, see or hear nothing. Guidance may come later in some other way.

For example, an answer can come by way of synchronicity. It may appear in something you overhear in line at the grocery store. It may come to you in a novel you happen to be reading, or something you see on TV.

Your answer might even seem to come from a tree or stream you are passing. Nature speaks to us in a myriad of ways, if we know how to listen.

In general, when you begin moving toward right action, you will feel a sense of flow and ease. This is an indication you're on the right track and that you're acting in resonance with your Soul.

Blocks to Receiving Guidance

Sometimes when you're waiting for an answer, you may run into parts of yourself that are blocking it. These may be aspects of yourself you are avoiding. Perhaps there's some part of you that is crying or is feeling angry.

It's important to listen to these upset voices in yourself. You don't need to know how to solve their laments, complaints or demands; you only need to listen to them with an open Heart and mind. This is what they want: to be heard and allowed to be who they are, feeling what they're feeling. And when you do, you'll find that they will eventually relax and begin to be interested, along with you, in what the answer to your question is.

However, once you believe you've received the answer you're seeking, you may still feel a resistance to the answer. If you can, calm yourself and simply sit quietly with the message you've received. Be careful not to reject it, or it may recede. Just let it float in your awareness and see what else may come to you to further your understanding and acceptance of this answer.

Right Action is Based in Truth

You will find that if your answer truly is right action, it is based in Truth. And your mind and your emotions, although perhaps rebellious at first, will begin to recognize the inherent authority of this Truth—and move into alignment with it. Your human self naturally recognizes the higher nature of Truth and will ultimately want to come into harmony with it.

You'll see that this is what you've been longing for: to be in sync with the higher Truth of who you are. And once you are, all decisions become infinitely easier to make.

Chapter 11
Raising Your Vibration

It could be said that the whole name of the game in the Ascension process is learning how to raise your vibration, as this is what needs to shift in order for you to be ready to experience fifth-dimensional consciousness. It's essential to raise your vibration to that of the Fifth Dimension and be able to remain resonating at that frequency no matter what happens.

So what does this mean? How can you know when you're experiencing a vibration that resonates with fifth-dimensional consciousness? Generally, it's when you are experiencing such feelings as love, joy, peace and harmony. It includes feelings of self confidence, self love and inner certainty. You feel happy and optimistic.

Most people can feel this way at times, but they generally can't sustain it. Usually this is because the feeling has been caused by outer circumstances of some kind—and outer circumstances always change.

In the Fifth Dimension, the high vibration you experience doesn't stem from reactions to outer circumstances; it's simply the frequency at which you naturally vibrate. And you remain there vibrating in that frequency in an ongoing way.

It's not that positive feelings and attitudes are good or right and negative ones are bad or wrong. (That's third-dimensional thinking.) It's just, very simply, that the vibrations that exist in the Fifth Dimension all resonate with joy, harmony, freedom, love and peace. And to remain there, you need to resonate with these same vibrations.

Staying Positive

One of the most powerful ways to raise your vibration is through thinking positive thoughts and experiencing positive emotions as much as possible. This, of course, is not easy to do, especially during these uncertain times. This is even more difficult because there's a huge amount of conditioning and habit from many, many lifetimes that may push against your efforts to bring new and positive energy into your life.

Mastering Your Thoughts & Emotions

And yet, this is exactly what is necessary: learning how to stay conscious of your thoughts and emotions to keep them positive. Fifth-dimensional consciousness involves being a master of your thoughts and emotions (and every word and action, as well).

However, this doesn't mean resisting negative thoughts and emotions and working to "get rid" of them. Nor does it mean following after them and allowing them to rule you. They are simply energy—you can let them be free to move in, around and out of you, without reacting to them or letting them take you over.

You actually don't have much control over what thoughts or emotions arise within you. They can seem to appear out of nowhere. But you *can* control whether you *keep* them going in your mind by continuing to dwell on them or not. And you can make the choice to shift your focus away from them, gently but firmly, to another more positive thought or emotion. You have the power to do this, whether you're aware of it or not.

If you really pay attention to what's happening in your mind, it may surprise you how often your thoughts turn to negative ideas and judgments, naturally bringing up negative emotions. You may find that you often go uncon-scious—even for hours at a time—in your thinking throughout the day, traveling down well-worn roads of fear, anger and judgment without being aware of it.

But if you have an intention to stay conscious and track your thoughts, you'll see where your mind goes. And you may be surprised not only at how many negative thoughts you have, but also how boring and repetitive they can be.

As you start tracking your thoughts and emotions, you can begin doing what you can to turn those of a low vibra-tion in a more positive direction. Sometimes repeating af-firmations or doing visualizations can help you do this. There are many books and other learning tools that teach various forms of "reprogramming" your mind in this way. Be careful not to dismiss them as simplistic positive think-ing tools. They point to a deep truth about how we create our reality and can be helpful in raising our vibration.

Don't Fall into Denial

This process of attempting to redirect thoughts and emotions can be tricky, however, because it's easy to simply push your negative thoughts and emotions into your unconscious—and then try to replace them with pos-itive thoughts. You can fall into denial, which ultimately is not helpful.

It's true you can be successful in the short run: you can think positive thoughts, which bring up positive emotions, and you can feel pretty good for a while. But sooner or later, what you've pushed into your unconscious is going to come up and bite you. Whatever you've avoided only gains more power over you.

In fact, whatever is in your unconscious has pretty much created your life today. That's why it's essential to not add any more to it. The important thing is to stay awake to what is passing through your consciousness—and take charge of it.

Greet Emotions Neutrally

As you become aware of lower vibrational thoughts and emotions arising, it's important to greet them in a neutral way. Acknowledge to yourself that these visitors are present. Be attentive to a habit that would have you resist them. Resistance will ultimately give them power over you. Stay as balanced and clear as you can as you notice their presence.

The key is to allow negativity, but to give it no energy. Instead, turn your thoughts to something more positive and allow the negativity to dissipate out of neglect.

Feel Your Feelings

If the feelings that arise are so powerful that you feel helpless to turn them around, it's important to give yourself permission to feel them. But be aware that you want to simply *feel* them—not indulge them and let them take you for a ride. It doesn't serve you to wallow in them. This is an art; it takes some concentration and practice to learn how to do this successfully.

An important part of this process is to watch that you don't keep jumping into your mind with a story about the problem and your emotions. This is an age-old habitual pattern to escape emotional pain. It's an attempt to *think* your emotions, rather than feel them. But it actually does nothing except keep you caught in the negative thinking, which continues to produce negative emotions.

If you find yourself thinking your emotions, rehashing the story and attempting to solve it, gently bring your attention back to the emotions you're experiencing and simply focus on feeling them. You can put your hand over the part of your body in which you feel the emotional pain. Breathe deeply into that area of your body.

If possible, see if you can even embrace and welcome the emotions. This can help you relax into a sense of relief and letting go. It's a way to be kind and compassionate with yourself and to practice being non-judgmental, accepting and allowing of all that you are.

In this process, however, be on the lookout for self-pity. "Poor Me" can creep in and entice you to begin indulging in "Helpless Victim" emotions. If you can keep focused, at a certain point you will likely see that you're relaxed enough with your difficult emotions that you can now focus on letting them go and shift your attention to a more positive perspective.

Once you feel an easing of the pressure of the uncomfortable energy you were feeling, see if you can shift your focus to something more satisfying and hopeful in your life, perhaps something you can be thankful for.

Once you're in a more balanced state, you can then turn back to the issue you started out with and find more loving and hopeful thoughts to think about it. And then begin feeling the emotions that emanate from those thoughts.

Learning to Manifest with Intention

Holding life-affirming thoughts and emotions is a powerful way to raise your vibration. But if you wish to lift it even further, you can focus on actually bringing new situations into your life that bring you joy. The best way to do this is through the principles of the Law of Attraction, an understanding that like attracts like.

Perhaps you're someone who has experimented in the past with manifesting through affirmations and visualization—both powerful tools—but have achieved only partial success with this process. Maybe you spent a short period of time each day thinking positively about something you wanted to manifest in your life, feeling positive feelings about it, and visualizing it clearly. And perhaps you repeated affirmations confirming it. All of this is helpful.

What you might not have realized, however, is that perhaps during the rest of the day, you were thinking limiting thoughts about what it was you were trying to manifest and feeling a sense of defeat or failure about it. You may not have made the connection, because a lot of negative rumination is based on age-old unconscious habit patterns.

The Universe Hears *Everything*

This may be why you weren't as successful in your manifesting as you might have wished. The universe hears *everything* you think, say, feel and believe—not just what you're consciously sending it.

So the short period of time a day you may have focused on your intent to manifest something could have been cancelled out by what you were thinking and feeling during the rest of the day. It will help to remember the simple truth that what you keep your attention on is what the universe responds to—period.

Another reason manifestation attempts often don't work is there's not enough energy or positive emotion to create the electromagnetic field that serves to attract what's being asked for.

In the Fifth Dimension and higher, the attraction mechanism is love. Not the emotion we know of as love in the Third Dimension—but a quality that has no opposite, a feeling that actually acts as a propellant, something that causes movement. We can experience this quality as a passion, an excitement, a radiance—an aliveness that is felt throughout our entire being.

Thoughts and Emotions Create our Reality

The thing to remember is that your thoughts and emotions create your reality, your experience of the world. Everything you're experiencing today—in your work, your relationships, your financial situation—all began as thoughts you once thought and then felt strong emotions about.

If you're not happy with what you're experiencing today, and you simply allow it all to keep happening while experiencing limiting and fearful thoughts and emotions about it, you will continue to create the same kinds of dissatisfying situations for the future. You will be doing this unconsciously and passively.

However, you can choose to respond differently to what you're not happy with today. You can take charge of the attraction mechanism by being intentional for a specific goal. As you keep your attention on your intention, you'll see that this focus can result in clear and desirable outcomes.

You Are Always Choosing

It's a matter of understanding that you are always choosing, whether it's intentionally or unintentionally, consciously or unconsciously. And whether you are choosing from a passive unconscious place or from a clear sense of purpose by keeping your attention on what you are asking to receive, you are choosing.

Happiness is a Choice

In fact, what you can discover is that happiness is actually a choice. Most of us have learned to believe that happiness is caused by outer circumstances, such as rewarding relationships, plenty of money, a satisfying job, good friends, etc. It can really look like these outer things are what are causing our happiness when we're experiencing it.

But we've all known people who seem to have all sorts of great things happening in their lives—and yet somehow manage to remain unhappy. And we may also know of people who have very little of what we'd consider "good fortune"—and yet they are cheerful and content most of the time.

This is because happiness truly is a choice we can make. Outer circumstances, no matter how fortunate or unfortunate they may be, always come and go; things are always changing. But our response to those circumstances is ultimately under our control. We can choose to be happy by simply having the intention to be so. We just need to find the place of happiness that exists inside us and decide to live from that place.

It may feel like there's no "place of happiness" inside you. But if you really think back in your life, you'll find this isn't true. See if you can remember a time in your life when you felt happy or content or joyful—some incident that happened in your past. (There's always at least one you've had!)

Bring back that memory. Remember the feelings you felt. Re-experience them fully now with your body and mind. Be aware when you do, of how your whole being lights up, how your body relaxes, and how your mind and emotions feel bathed in a sense of well-being.

In remembering all this and re-experiencing it, you now have access to the feeling of happiness. You can feel it now, in the present moment. And you can focus on it, give energy to it, grow it bigger inside of you.

Once you do this a few times in remembering that time of happiness, you won't have to remember it anymore in order to access the feeling of happiness. You will have created a space within you now that knows and fully experiences it. And at that point, you can simply practice moving to that space within you that knows this happiness—and live your life from there. It takes some time to develop this, but it may actually be surprising at how quickly you can create this space in you that deeply feels a living happiness.

The interesting thing is that as you do this, you will begin attracting more and more happiness to your life. The universe will respond with more of the same, perhaps even adding outer reasons to match and enhance your joyful state of being.

Your inner state of consciousness is one thing you can be in charge of. If you want to feel happy, joyful, peaceful, free—all those wonderful states of being—you can, simply through the practice of choice and intention.

And the more you do this, the greater mental clarity you'll have. You'll be able to quiet your mind more easily. Your body will feel more energetic and healthy. You'll see that, effortlessly, you have created a space for the passion of your true Being to begin expressing itself. You'll be well on your way to experiencing fifth-dimensional consciousness.

And because you are connected to all that exists on Earth, every happy, loving, peaceful thought and feeling you experience will actually be contributing to the transformation of consciousness occurring in all of humanity.

Be Your Own Teacher

There are numerous ways to develop positive and uplifting vibrations in yourself, including specific techniques and guided meditations offered by many teachers today. If you feel drawn to a certain teacher or body of teachings, then trust your intuition on this.

Almost everyone needs help in raising their vibration, given the thousands of years of functioning at a third-dimensional vibration, and tools offered by those further along on the path can be very helpful. But it's important to not give your power away to teachers.

It is especially important at this time to become your own inner teacher and authority. Experiment with tools that others offer and see if you feel they help to free you. If not, then know they're not for you. Stay in charge and responsible for yourself and your Ascension.

Chapter 12
Simple Ways to Quickly Raise your Vibration

Raising your vibration through staying positive and learning to manifest with intention is essential in eventually sustaining a high vibration. This takes some concentration and practice.

There are also some quick and simple practices you can develop that will be helpful in raising your vibration—especially if you're in a situation in which you need something quick to lift yours spirits.

The Magic of Gratitude

One of the fastest ways to raise your vibration is to move into a consciousness of gratitude. Gratitude automatically opens you to a more joyful and satisfying experience of life. It's also one of the best ways to experience a sense of on-going peace, centeredness and connection. When you truly feel gratitude, you cannot experience suffering at the same time; the two experiences cannot co-exist.

However, moving into a feeling of gratitude is often not that easy. You might feel so consumed by pain or irritability at how life is "treating" you that it's difficult to simply shift out of the unhappy experience you're in to focus on what you might be thankful for.

If this is the case, it's best not to try to push your negative feelings aside and attempt to move to a feeling of gratitude. As described in the last chapter, you need to feel your feelings first—without any judgment you may have of them.

Acknowledge that you're in a difficult space and allow that to be okay, just for now. Face and feel the emotions, without identifying with them. It may be helpful to focus on the part of your body that's feeling the emotion and breathe deeply into it. Once you feel an easing of the pressure of the energy you were feeling, see if you can shift your focus to something you can be thankful for.

If it's hard at the moment to think of anything significant, think of anything at all—even something as simple as the fact that you remembered your umbrella and it's started raining. Or you've got eggs in the fridge and that's exactly what you feel like eating. Say "Thank you, thank you!" to the universe. Even add "Thank you—more please!" and watch to see the magic that can happen within you.

Feeling grateful for mundane things like this can begin to shift your awareness. Once you are successful in feeling gratitude for the smaller things, then a pathway opens up to begin looking for more important things in your life to feel thankful for.

The greater your gratitude is for the important things in your life, the greater the feeling of peace and joy that can come into your life. In fact, if you can simply remember the magic of gratitude, your passage through difficult experiences in your Ascension journey will be a lot smoother.

The Living Vibration of Words

All words have living vibrations. A valuable tool offered by Jim Self is to repeat to yourself words with positive vibrations, so that your own vibration eventually comes into resonance with that of the words. This is somewhat different from repeating affirmations, in that it's a matter of focusing on the vibration in a particular word, rather than on a concept that words may be pointing to.

"Gratitude", for example, is a word with a very high vibration. In fact, if it ever feels too hard to shift into gratitude for even small, mundane things, then try simply saying the word "gratitude" to yourself, over and over again, at least 10-15 times.

You may be surprised at how even just repeating this powerful word can begin to shift your experience away from pain and negativity and help to raise your vibration.

Other words can also serve you in this way. For instance, try saying and feeling words like Joy, Ease, Happy, or Confidence over and over again, or whatever it is you'd like to be feeling. (Nouns or adjectives work equally well—use what works for you.)

This can sound overly simplistic. You may wonder how just repeating a word could possibly do anything significant within you. But try it and see for yourself what happens.

Anchoring Positive Feeling into Words

As was discussed in the last chapter, one thing that's helpful in doing this is to remember a time when you experienced the feeling you'd like to be experiencing now. Remember it clearly in detail—where you were, what the weather was like, if there were others with you, how your body felt—and all the good feelings that arose out of that experience.

Then anchor all these good feelings into the word now in current time, so that every time you repeat it, those feelings come present within you. Eventually you won't have to go back to that memory to feel the power of the positive vibration in you—it will have been infused into the word itself and you'll feel it automatically in just saying it.

As you repeat a word, fully experience it. Let it fill your whole body. If you make a practice of repeating these high vibrational words, you will be infusing your body and your aura with vibrant living colors. With practice and repetition, these vibrations will remain with you and affect your everyday experience of yourself and your life.

Powerful Phrases

Certain phrases are also very powerful in raising your vibration quickly. Teacher Matt Kahn emphasizes that simply saying the words "I love you" to yourself over and over again will not only raise your vibration, it will break down inner barriers that cause you to resist love.

The phrase "God bless you, I love you" is also an amazingly powerful statement to repeat inwardly when you're having difficulty with another person or feeling hostility from them. Just saying these words keeps you in a high vibration, and it also acts as a protective shield against another person's anger or hostility. And quite surprisingly, it often has a positive effect on the other person, as well, who will likely have no clue as to what you're doing!

Yet another powerful phrase that can raise your vibration is "I like me." Try saying this one out loud a number of times and feel what it does to you.

Experiencing Wonder

Another way to raise your vibration is to shift your attention from your thinking mind and the story of your life—and into that place inside yourself that is innocent and child-like, that part of you that looks at life with wonder and curiosity.

Take a moment to look closely at what's around you in a fresh way, as if you've never seen it before. Give yourself the time to be totally present with something you're looking at. Feel your awareness soften and expand. You may discover that you have the capacity to pull back the filter of your mind and just look at it directly, as it is, without any thought about it.

This may be easiest to do when out in nature. Every leaf, flower, tree or insect holds infinite mysteries you can only begin to understand with your Heart. Become still inside and just feel into the silence. Experience the pure sense of wonder that arises.

You can actually experience a sense of wonder anywhere, with anyone or anything—even inside a room with lots of noisy people talking on their cell phones or engaged in tense interactions with each other. Step back and just watch the scene, as if coming upon it as a curious child for the first time.

Experience the wonder of the human being. Every person, even someone who seems unconscious and caught in third-dimensional negativity, is actually wondrous to behold, if you can just see them with new and fresh eyes—without judgment, without evaluating what is attractive or unattractive to you. You can see them just as they are—clearly and directly. And marvel at all that a human being is and can do—or even that such a complex creature can exist.

Even something as mundane as your hand can be something wondrous to behold. Again, move beyond your mind and allow yourself to just gaze at it, free from any thoughts about it—and see what is actually there. You may find it to be an amazing and fascinating creation!

Seek Beauty

When you're vibrating at a high vibration, you automatically begin seeing beauty all around you. This is because beauty itself resonates at a high vibration.

But there may be times during the planet's transition to the Fifth Dimension when it will seem that everywhere you look, you see sorrow, pain, struggle or injustice. Everything may be pointing to the ugliness in life, either inside yourself or in your outer world. When you focus on all of this, especially on your helplessness to make much of a difference, of course, your vibration will drop automatically.

Life in the Third Dimension has always been fraught with suffering of one kind or another. It's inherent in the nature of third-dimensional consciousness, which is both very limited and out of touch with Truth. Being caught in this consciousness can create a great heaviness in your heart.

It's important when you're experiencing this darker side of life to seek beauty anywhere you can find it; beauty brings solace to a heavy heart. Become aware that, despite the ugliness that exists here, there is also great beauty that is never far away.

You can almost always find beauty in Nature. You can also find beauty in all human beings, if you seek to glimpse the Soul. Children are most transparent in their beauty, but all people emanate it if you look closely enough. Music and art in all forms also can offer the nurturing energy of beauty.

But don't forget to seek beauty within yourself, as well. See if you can move past any judgments you may have of yourself and find the unique beauty that resides within you.

As you ascend higher and higher toward fifth-dimensional consciousness, you will find that beauty can so affect you that even the simplest thing can move you to tears of joy: a bird alighting on a branch, a flower opening to the sun, a child taking its first steps.

Calling in the Holy Spirit

Yet another way to raise your vibration quickly is to call in a particular source of celestial Light from the highest dimensions known as the Holy Spirit. Sometimes if you're feeling overwhelmed by your emotional state, it can be difficult to remember or practice the different keys you've learned to move yourself into a higher vibration.

In this case, the simple act of calling in the Light of the Holy Spirit can be an easy one to remember. And it can be enormously powerful. All you need to do is ask that this Light fill you, surround you and protect you for the highest good of all concerned—and it will come.

When you ask for it, feel open for Light to appear in and around you. If you are visual, you may see this Light as a radiant goldish-white light. Or you may simply feel its soft and soothing energy as it enters your being. You may also experience a deep love flowing into you, one that gently washes away sorrow and grief.

Allow yourself to melt into it, surrender to its caress. You will feel your vibration lifting and your perspective on what you were previously experiencing to shift into being more hopeful and optimistic.

You may also sense with this Light the presence of such beings as Jesus (also known as Yeshua or Sananda), Quan Yin, Mother Mary or other celestial beings that are known for their powerful healing love. If you feel a resonance with these beings, you can turn to them to gain solace from their compassion, as well as wisdom from their guidance.

You actually don't have to wait till you're desperate to call in the Holy Spirit. This is a practice you can do regularly, in any situation, to gradually raise the vibration of your auric field. You may notice that people seem to sense it with you. They might even mention that they feel or see a new "glow" about you.

Chapter 13
Experiencing Oneness

Perhaps one of the most powerful experiences we have had during our long sojourn in the Third Dimension is that of perceiving and believing ourselves to be entities that are separate from each other. Having lost our understanding of the nature of reality since the Fall of Consciousness, we have focused on what we could perceive with just our five senses—that our bodies are separate and unconnected—and have thus concluded that we are separate and unconnected to each other.

Many of us awakening into higher fourth and fifth-dimensional consciousness are having powerful experiences of seeing this sense of separation and disconnection with each other to be illusion. We are experiencing the reality of oneness that inherently exists with all of humanity. Although we have perhaps always intuited that this oneness exists, we are now having deep experiences of it, realizing that not only are we all connected—we are all really one consciousness.

Overcoming Judgmental Attitudes

You have likely had these experiences yourself: deep within you, you know the oneness that exists among all human beings—and indeed with all that exists. Perhaps you have felt a profound love and compassion for people with this, no matter who they are or what they do.

If so, it has probably distressed you when a sense of separation continues to arise within you at times, especially when it comes along with a sense of judgment.

Judgment is a habit that can be very hard to break. Perhaps you've attempted to be less judgmental in your life
but have found it difficult to completely overcome. As
much as you may not want to judge, your mind may often
seem to have a mind of its own.

It can be especially difficult if you've observed so much
of what's wrong with the world: violence, wars, injustice,
lack of compassion. And from what you've experienced,
perhaps you've naturally drawn the conclusion that there
exist "bad" people who are greedy, selfish and uncaring
who perpetuate all that's wrong with the world, and there
are "good" loving people who align with peace, justice,
and harmony and justice.

It's even more difficult to avoid judgment if you believe
the "bad" people have pretty much been in control of the
world forever, keeping humanity suppressed by starting
wars, ignoring the poor and downtrodden, and preventing
justice. Maybe you've even believed that these people
should be exposed and brought down. It may feel natural
to jump into the camp of those fighting against the "black
hats" and to be glad when they've been brought down.

The Attitude of Spiritual Superiority

There's probably something in you that recognizes that
your longing for kindness and caring emanates from a
deep spiritual knowing within you. But a problem can
arise if you develop an attitude of spiritual superiority, an
attitude of "againstness" and separation from other people. This feeds struggle and dissension both within yourself personally and in your world.

To move into a fifth-dimensional consciousness, it's
important to be aware when you're judging others. As the
old saying goes, if you want peace, unity and love in the
world—you need to start with yourself. In the Fifth Dimension, there is no separation, no sense of "us against

them". Indeed, there is no right and wrong—all polarities are non-existent.

When we're living in alignment with Truth, we know that everyone is a Soul journeying through this challenging experience of incarnation on planet Earth. Everyone is attempting, consciously or unconsciously, to find their way Home. It's true that some people look like they've taken some twists and turns along the way, apparently getting caught in more negativity and darkness than others. But that's the only difference—they're simply not yet very awake to the truth of who they are.

Every one of us is doing the very best we can with what we know and understand. We're all in this together, bumbling along, trying to find our way through the density, separation and fear here. Within all the confusion, disappointment and suffering, it's important to remember there is a divine plan unfolding that is beyond the understanding of the rational mind. So to hold judgments against anyone or anything often simply points to our ignorance.

This doesn't mean we should never do anything to try to set things on a better path or bring a situation into a better alignment with Truth as we see it. If we see something that we can assist with or someone who could use our help—of course, we should take the opportunity to do these things. It's probably part of the divine plan that we do so.

The point is that it's important to do the things that feel right without the attitudes of againstness or superiority. And to also be aware that "feeling sorry" for people may be just another way for the ego to feel superior.

All this can sometimes be tricky, as old attitudes and feelings can so easily slip in and motivate us to speak or act in a self-righteous or superior way. But being aware of them can help us steer clear of these pitfalls.

Judging People We Love

Judgment can also show up with people we love. In fact, we may find ourselves judging most harshly those who are most beloved to us.

Judgment on this level seems to come about naturally whenever stress appears in our everyday life, when things aren't going the way we want them to. It's easy to lash out in judgment at someone we know will understand and forgive us. The mind just automatically seems to do this.

So what can you do to stop this automatic reaction? How can you cease the tendency of the mind to judge people, even those you love?

You're Hurting Yourself

The first thing is to really understand why judging others is harmful. It's not because it's morally wrong. It's not even primarily because it may hurt the people you're judging.

It's because when you're in judgment, you're hurting yourself. It separates you from another person, and this denies the oneness that actually exists between the two of you. It also lowers your vibration, keeping you at the level where separation, conflict and suffering exist.

At the same time, be careful of feeling shame or self-blame if you find yourself in judgment of someone. Don't fall into thinking you're a "bad" or "unspiritual" person. The truth is you're simply not seeing the truth clearly.

Telling yourself you "should" be compassionate and understanding is rarely effective. This may work for a short while (shame can be a powerful motivator), but it usually doesn't work in the long run. Judgment will continue to show up and you can only push it away so much before it backfires on you.

Why We Judge

What's important to understand is why people judge in the first place. It's actually quite simple: When we're judging someone, it indicates we're not feeling very good about ourselves, we're judging ourselves about something. And we're trying to do something to make ourselves feel better.

Here's how it works: When you're judging yourself, this brings on a feeling of low self worth. This in turn brings in a feeling of loneliness and separation, which then generates a feeling of wanting to strike out at someone else with judgment to try and ease the pain.

Very simply, judging is an attempt to alleviate a feeling of inferiority and inadequacy. It's the mind's way of trying to feel superior to counteract this feeling. The unconscious belief that's present is: "If I align myself with those I deem to be superior, more spiritual, more successful, more intelligent than others—then I too can feel superior, spiritual, successful, intelligent. If I can feel morally right and better than rich, greedy, lazy, aggressive, stupid, ugly, uncaring (fill in the blank) people, then I can feel better about myself—I can respect and like myself more."

Judging is also often an attempt to alleviate a feeling of loneliness and separation. The belief is: "If I can align with another person or group opposing another group, I can feel less lonely, separate, left out. I can feel a sense of identity of belonging to a group."

But, of course, it doesn't really work in the end. When you judge others, it doesn't make you feel any better in an ongoing way. It doesn't resolve the underlying issue.

If you're wondering if all this is true, think about it for a moment: When you're feeling good about yourself and you're feeling connected to others, do you tend to be judgmental about anyone?

Compassion for Yourself

When you find yourself being judgmental, it won't do you any good to berate yourself or to try to be accepting and compassionate about someone. Instead, *turn toward yourself with compassion.*

Realize that your judgmentalness is just a sign that you're not feeling good about yourself, that you're judging yourself in some way—and what you're trying to do is feel better. You're trying to feel a bond with others you respect and like, so you can feel less lonely and separate.

Then you have the opportunity to gently explore how you're judging yourself and see how you might stop. You can see if there are ways in which you might create a greater sense of self-worth and feel a bond with people you like and respect in a more effective and healthy way than through judgment.

Eventually, when you start turning from being judgmental about people, you may begin to find it actually painful if you hear yourself saying something negative about someone. You may even feel pain when you hear someone else being judgmental about another person.

This is a sign of a growing awareness of the oneness that exists among all of us, the truth that all of humanity is really like one multi-celled organism. Your response to someone else's pain is like the automatic response of your hand when you bump your knee—it immediately reaches out to your knee to comfort it.

Relating to Others on a Soul Level

Indeed, once we step away from judgment of others, we find ourselves living more and more at the frequency of the Soul and developing the ability to relate to others from the Soul level—an experience of the higher Fourth and Fifth Dimensions.

It can sometimes be easy to have this experience with someone who immediately feels like an old friend when we initially meet them. We can readily experience them from a higher consciousness; we recognize them as someone we've known forever on the Soul level, and it's clear that we're both Souls who have come together in love and respect.

It can be a lot harder at times to see our familiar loved ones as clearly—our family members, intimate partners, and close friends. This is because when we come together in important relationships like this, we usually do so because we've agreed to incarnate together so as to help each other to grow and learn, and to work through karma.

And so we can easily trigger and bring out the worst in each other. We can find ourselves in judgment and separation, and it's difficult to remember that we're here together because of a deep Soul love we have for each other.

It can be helpful to learn how to move into Soul awareness when you're having challenges with a loved one and you're caught in judgment, hostility and defensiveness. When you move out of your limited self into a higher Soul consciousness, you can see life very differently, and you can naturally experience your deep love for the person.

Moving into Soul awareness when you're feeling angry and in separation with someone is not always easy. So it's helpful to practice it when you're not currently feeling triggered by them.

At some point when you're feeling quiet and centered, bring this person into your awareness. Feel into them as a human being. Be aware of the difficulty you have with them, how they drive you crazy or push your buttons. Experience your wanting to push them away, reject them, or change them.

Realize that this is just normal human behavior. There's nothing to be ashamed of—it's how two human beings used to living in the Third Dimension generally act and react when there are differences present. Be compassionate with yourself.

Once you're feeling accepting of your own feelings of resistance and judgment, see if you can now reach into yourself to move into a higher consciousness. Call in the presence of your Soul and feel it embrace you. In doing this, you may realize that your Soul is not some small thing inside your body as many people perceive it to be— it is actually a presence that surrounds and envelops you. Your body resides within it.

See if you can merge with this presence. You may feel a sense of expansion or spaciousness with this—a feeling that you're not confined to your body and mind. It's an open, relaxed feeling. It's light and free.

As you do this, notice how your mind quiets. You may have a sense of the eternal, of no-time. You may be aware that you have access in this space to the knowledge of your past lives and possible futures. You may become aware of the presence of God. Feel your connection to this presence, and to all of life, everywhere. Feel the consciousness of love.

As you reach this higher, clearer space within you, bring the person you've been having difficulty with into that space with you. What is it like to see and feel them there? Can you sense them as a Soul? What is your relationship with them at this level, Soul to Soul? What do you experience, what do you understand about them and your relationship with them? Can you experience the deep love you have for them—and have probably felt for many, many lifetimes?

What would it be like to be able to relate to this person from this level of Soul consciousness all the time? Even when they're being annoying or hostile?

The Experience of True Oneness

In practicing now to relate to people Soul to Soul, you are preparing yourself for your experience in the Fifth Dimension. And, of course, it also makes life a lot more enjoyable and uplifting on your journey there. A greater peace and balance can come into your life. You feel more fully connected to all of humanity.

And with this, an exciting experience might then begin unfolding—one that is even deeper than the feeling of connectedness. It's a knowing of actual oneness, that everyone—indeed all that exists—is truly just one consciousness. Not many consciousnesses connected to each other—but one consciousness having many different experiences.

And you are that one consciousness.

Chapter 14
Your Spiritual Mission

If you feel called to take part in helping with the transition of the planet into the Fifth Dimension, you can be certain that there is something specific you have volunteered to do during these times. You have likely signed up to join the "Light Team" here to help raise the vibration of humanity in your own unique way, using your own unique skills, talents, and experiences. You have taken on what's called a "spiritual mission".

Spiritual Activists

Some spiritual missions involve a lot of outer, physical activity. They revolve around the creation and building of new structures, systems, and social formations that will be coming into being on the new Earth emerging in the Fifth Dimension.

If you feel drawn to go out in the world to create greater justice and peace, you likely have a mission as a spiritual activist. You may feel that being politically or socially active is how you're going to be expressing your mission. Or you may wish to set up new structures for people to feel more empowered and more involved in creating better lives for themselves. There are a myriad of ways you can discover to do this.

One thing that can be challenging if you are someone wanting to create new political or social structures is the tendency to fall into the third-dimensional consciousness of condemning the people trying to hold onto power in the old structures.

Yes, if they aren't willing to change, they probably need to step down and make way for the new consciousness coming to the planet of love, harmony justice and understanding. But focusing on making people wrong will not assist you in bringing in this new consciousness. Do your best, rather, to focus on creating new forms and ways of being, rather than on those that are defective, destructive or ineffective.

Part of your job as a spiritual activist is to help lead other people in that new conscious direction. Often people don't know how to do anything except complain about what's not right and about how wrongly they're being treated by others or systems in power. With a higher vibration of empowerment and positive focus, you can guide them away from perceiving themselves as victims and into creating what's in their highest interest.

Frequency Holders

Other missions are more subtle and not as visible. People who have signed up for these are sometimes known as "frequency holders". These are people who are quietly holding a high vibration and sending light and love everywhere on the planet through prayer, meditation, visualization and inner focus.

Frequency holders are not as drawn to be physically active in creating a new world, and so they are not easily known by others. But their work is equally important. They create a "battery" of energy that the activists can access to gain strength and power to do their own work. Both groups together are necessary for bringing about the planetary Shift.

If you believe you're a frequency holder, know that your job involves more than simply meditating in your old accustomed way, or occasionally holding light and love for people. It may be something much more. If it hasn't already been shown to you, at some point you will be guided to use the energetic processes you know to support what is needed on the planet in its transition to the Fifth Dimension.

Your Life Has Prepared You

If you don't yet know what your spiritual mission is, don't despair. It will soon start getting clear. It will probably not be a surprise what it turns out to be. In one way or another, you have been preparing for it all your life.

At some point you may actually see how everything you've experienced in your life so far all fits together in a great puzzle. This puzzle can reveal a map of how you have been prepared to accomplish your spiritual mission in the coming years in the best way possible.

When you discover your mission, which is actually simply a *remembering* of what you signed up for, you'll see that there have been themes—interwoven threads—throughout your life forming the fabric of your spiritual mission. These have appeared not only in the work you've done and in what you've studied and experienced along your spiritual path; they've also shown up in your childhood experiences, your relationships, and your dreams.

One way to become aware of your specific mission is to take time to move inward and speak to your inner guidance "team" about your mission. Ask for help in clarifying it. Ask for what you think you need in order to manifest it and get yourself going. Nothing is too small or mundane to ask for. Know that whatever your mission is, you are fully equipped to accomplish it, and that you will be given what you need.

Feel into new people coming present in your life at this time or those who may be moving more closely into your energy field. Are they soul mission partners for you? Is there a dynamic energy vortex that seems to form when you're with them? If so, explore with them what you think it might be about.

The nature of your soul mission has been held safely within a sacred space in your Heart since birth. It may be time now to access it—and to explore what your unique role may be on the global team now helping to awaken humanity.

Patience

If nothing seems to be moving forward at this time in either discovering or starting your mission, you may have to accept that the timing isn't quite right yet and you need to practice patience. You might believe you see clearly what you're here to do and that you're ready to do it; but perhaps there is still need for preparation so that all may be in place for you to move forward with it.

This may be preparation that needs to take place within you—emotional work, clearing of negative energy, or continued learning. Or the preparation could be that which is needed by others you will be involved with in doing your mission. Or it may simply involve right timing in other ways.

No matter the reason for the feeling of "hold up", trust that all is as it should be.   Ask inwardly if there is anything you need to be aware of that may be in the way of manifesting your vision. Ask for help in raising both your vibration and your perspective on the matter.

If you look at yourself from a greater distance, you can probably see your progress more clearly and understand why more time is currently needed before you can begin your mission. Or, in standing back from your ideas of what it should look like, you may even discover that, in fact, you've already in one way or another begun it.

Trust that at the right time your mission will be revealed to you. Remember, your Higher Self is running the show. Know that It understands well what you're here to do, what it is you need to do it, and when to bring things together into your life so you can do it. It knows perfect timing.

When it is right, all will be in place, and you will be ready. Synchronicities will occur, everything will line up, and you will see the perfection of it all. And should you be wondering if you'll know your mission when it shows up, fear not—you will know it because you will not be able to NOT do it.

In a way, it will take you over, and you will willingly give yourself to it. Aligning yourself with your mission will give you such a deep sense of Soul-fulfillment, you will have no doubt that this is what you are here to do and be.

Awakening of Psychic Abilities

Part of your mission may involve a deepening of your sensitivity to people's energies to be able to assist them in their Ascension process. If so, you may begin to experience subtle energy patterns when you're with others and knowing intuitively what they mean.

Perhaps your ability to read someone's mind or to know clearly what they're feeling will become more pronounced. Or you'll have brief moments of seeing a past life with them or seeing colors in their aura and know what they mean about the person.

These new abilities can be very exciting to experience. Until recently, these types of skills have been relatively rare. But more and more people are awakening to these psychic skills, and in the times to come, they will be more commonplace. The powerful frequencies currently coming onto the Earth are opening and activating centers in many people's brains.

With some practice, you may be able to develop these skills or further expand them, if you feel called to do so. You may be able to do much good in helping others when using them. Do remember however, that with psychic abilities there comes much responsibility. With awareness of what someone's thoughts or feelings are, you must discern whether it's appropriate to share with them what you've perceived.

Sometimes what's best is to not invade a person's privacy—to actually say and do nothing with the information you receive. Of course, if someone should ask you what you see or sense, it may be appropriate. But even then, ask within first to see if it is and how best to express it.

Be aware that your ego may want to co-opt your abilities and claim them for its own. Watch to ensure you don't start using them for selfish gain or to simply boost your feeling of self-worth. And also watch to see that your ego doesn't start dimming your vision with its own perspectives and desires.

When used clearly and responsibly, your skills at seeing truth beneath the surface could prove to be a great gift—both to you and others around you. Use them wisely, and you may be of great assistance to many people.

Communication with Beings from Other Kingdoms

Another ability that may open up for you is having close contact and communication with beings from other realms, such as the angelic, animal and elemental kingdoms.

This can be very exciting and rewarding as you experience "remembering" the close contact you once had in ancient times with these beings. At one time, before the Fall of Consciousness, we all had free access and clear communication with these beings and forces.

If this ability begins opening up for you, it may be a pointer to what your spiritual mission may be. The beings in these other realms may be "mission partners" you'll be working with in helping to wake people up to their existence and true nature. Feel into this possibility and see what may come present for you.

Chapter 15
Returning Home

The journey into the Fifth Dimension through these "Transitional Times" can be a challenging one. It's requiring us to change much more rapidly than we've ever had to change before. And the changes we're making can at times feel enormous. We are needing to let go of much of what we've based our whole sense of identity on, as well as a lot of what helped us feel secure in life.

For many of us, the Ascension process also involves outer losses—relationships, financial security, and long-held careers. It requires us to live from a consciousness of deep trust in the Unknown and to venture forth without our usual, familiar modes of operating. All of this can be frightening, especially as we see our world around us also morphing into what may at times look like chaos.

However, if we stand back and view what's happening both in ourselves and in the world from a higher perspective, we can see that this journey is one we can make with tremendous excitement.

We are letting go of old, dysfunctional structures and patterns that are based in separation, ignorance and suffering. We are releasing distorted perceptions and emotions that have been holding us back for thousands of years from experiencing all of who we are and can be—powerful, multi-dimensional beings. We are shifting back into full consciousness. We are becoming Heart-centered beings guided by the love and joy of our inherent spiritual natures.

At some point in the not-too-distant future, we will be living in a world we have only dreamed of, one in which a knowing of oneness, peace and harmony reigns. People will communicate with love, kindness, respect and understanding. And the Earth will once again be honored.

What will help us when things get rough during these Transitional Times is remembering the big picture of what is happening. We are in a grand birthing process. Rather than distressing about what is falling apart and disappearing, we can focus on what is being born.

We can keep centered in the love in our Hearts. We can keep focused on a consciousness of trust. We can begin visioning and creating right now the New Earth. As we do this, we can greatly affect what is going on all across the planet. If enough of us keep focused on love and joy and keep adding our own light to the waves of Light streaming onto the Earth, we can help to manifest the world so many of us have yearned for.

Already we can see the planetary consciousness rising. People world-wide are waking up to who they truly are. Just a fraction of us need to keep lifting our vibrations, and we can eventually impact the entire world. What each of us does within our own consciousness truly has an effect on the consciousness of the collective. And those of us awakening now can create a bridge for others to awaken and cross along with us to fifth-dimensional consciousness.

What a privilege to be alive on the Earth during these times! What joy to be part of this grand plan to help bring the planet and humanity back into a consciousness of love, truth and freedom.

If we can keep focused on this vision, we can stay centered, balanced and joyful as we travel along the sometimes rocky terrain of the Fourth Dimension—making our way, at long last, back Home.

Resources

1. Beckow, Steve: www.goldenageofgaia.com
2. Benedicte, Meg: www.newearthcentral.com
3. Bishop, Karen: *Down into Up*,
   http://ascensioncorner.wordpress.com/
4. Cota-Robles, Patricia: www.eraofpeace.org/
5. Day, Christine: *Pleiadian Principles for Living*,
   http://www.christinedayonline.com/
6. Dillon, Linda: http://counciloflove.com/
7. Hamilton, Craig:
   http://integralenlightenment.com/home.php
8. Hoffman, Brenda:
   http://lifetapestrycreations.wordpress.com/
9. Hoffman, Jennifer: http://enlighteninglife.com
10. Jones, Aurelia Louise: *Telos*, Vols. 1, 2 3
11. Kahn, Matt: http://www.truedivinenature.com/
12. Kenyon, Tom: http://tomkenyon.com/
13. Marx-Hubbard, Barbara:
    http://barbaramarxhubbard.com/
14. Melkizedek, Drunvalo: *Serpent of Light*,
    http://www.drunvalo.net/
15. Self, Jim: *What Do You Mean the Third Dimension is Going Away?* www.masteringalchemy.com/
16. Ward, Suzi:
    http://www.matthewbooks.com/mattsmessage.htm/

Acknowledgments

I am immeasurably grateful to the many teachers and guides I have been gifted to know throughout the years who have pointed the way for me along my sometimes rocky path of awakening. But most memorable in earlier years include John-Roger, Papaji, Ramana Maharshi, Ramesh Balsekar, Nisargadatta, Gangaji, and Adyashanti. In more recent years, I give enormous thanks to both Dell Morris and Jim Self for their clarity, understanding and guidance about the Ascension process.

I wish to acknowledge and give my heartfelt thanks to Marjorie Bair for her editing consultation of this book and also for her unflagging support of me as I wrote it. Her own knowledge and personal experience with the Ascension process has been invaluable to me. And having her as a close and loving companion along the path in these latter years has meant a great deal to me.

I also wish to acknowledge Shri Estes, my Soul-friend of many years, who has traveled with me through uncountable periods of intense inner growth and life changes. At times, it was her love, support and profound depth of understanding that helped me to keep my equilibrium and sense of humor through some of the most difficult events in my life.

Other dear friends and buddies along the ascension path have included Georgia Dow, Grace Galzagorry, and Pat and Bob Basham—all of whom I have much love and gratitude for. Their sharing of their experiences during these years of Ascension have been very valuable to me, both personally and in writing this book. In addition, I have deep gratitude for Lauren Matthews and Linda Miller, both who have supported me with deep love for many years throughout my years of awakening.

I wish to especially acknowledge my daughter, who has an enormous capacity for listening with love, patience and astute awareness whenever I ramble on about everything happening in my life. At times, her quiet inner beauty and ethereal essence take my breath away, leaving me wondering where in the universe she has dropped in from.

And lastly, I want to thank my dear Pleiadian Soul companions, A Ram and Sha Rohn for their support and guidance through my Ascension process. In particular, I am immensely grateful to them for allowing me to experience a merging intimacy with them that far surpasses any love I've ever known on this physical level. The possibilities they show me of how life can be in the Fifth Dimension have often pulled me through some dark inner passages occurring along my Ascension journey and have also given me a profound experience of remembering myself as an expansive multidimensional being.

About the Author

Vidya Frazier has studied with a number of spiritual teachers from both western and eastern traditions for over 40 years. In 1993, she felt called to India to visit the spiritual master, Papaji. Upon returning, she wrote *The Art of Letting Go–A Pathway to Inner Freedom* and began offering individual sessions, groups and workshops based on this book.

In 2007, she was invited to attend the Oneness University in India and was initiated as a Oneness Blessing Facilitator. She returned and offered the blessing to hundreds of people. Since then, she has studied with Quantum Healer Dell Morris, and teacher and author Jim Self.

The present focus in her work is assisting people to find their way with clarity and ease through the powerful energies of the Shift of consciousness that is now occurring across the planet. She also assists people in discovering their spiritual purpose in life and stepping more fully into expressing it.

Drawing on thirty-five years as a licensed psychotherapist, hypnotherapist, and spiritual guide, as well as on her own spiritual awakening experiences, Vidya serves as a unique bridge between the worlds of psychology and spiritual awakening.

Contact Vidya at www.vidyafrazier.com.

Printed in the USA
CPSIA information can be obtained
at www.ICGtesting.com
LVHW040729230324
775212LV00007B/387

9 781622 876297